becoming

DEBT-FREE

becoming
DEBT-FREE

how we paid off $105,000
and discovered the power of personal
finances
(and the ways you can, too)

MONICA REINHARD

Becoming DEBT-FREE
How We Paid off $105,000 and Discovered the Power of Personal
Finances
(and the ways you can, too)

ISBN: 978-1-6936-1764-5

Cover and interior design by Jason Reinhard
Printed in the United States of America
Published by Monica & Jason Reinhard

To our parents:

Monica's: George Miller & Mindy Long
Jason's: Chris & Debbie Reinhard

Without each one of you our successes and accomplishments
wouldn't be possible.
Your lifelong encouragement, support, and love are the most
valuable gifts and securities we will never have to pay for.

The first few times someone told me I should write a book about paying off our loans and getting out of debt, I laughed and said, "yeah, right," because of course it was a joke – they're always joking, right?

Nobody actually writes a book when they're told to write a book. And nobody reads the book they say should be written. It's just a thing we say: *you should write a book about X. I would read that book about Y.* Like losing weight or looking for a new job: *I'll get to it one day.*

But sometimes when we hear a suggestion enough times, one certain instance sticks. I know the moment that one instance stuck for me.

Someone said I should write the book and I said, "I know, right," *but maybe this time they weren't joking and maybe this time I would actually consider what they said*, and the moment passed but the gears in my brain kept turning.

So here's the book. Here's our story. It is not a unique one, but every word is true.

I will tell you now – I am not a finance expert. My husband Jason is not a finance expert. We don't have business degrees (or degrees we even use, to be honest), we aren't millionaires (*yet*), and we don't have all the answers. At this point of writing I worked at a coffee bar and Jason was an assistant plant manager for a concrete products company.

We're just two millennials who racked up a hive-inducing amount of student loan debt and decided to figure out how to get rid of it as quickly as possible.

It changed our lives, but we aren't special because of it. We aren't perfect and we don't follow every money rule found online and taught by financial gurus. We do things you may not agree with or want to do yourself, and we don't do things you might think are necessary and match your personal preferences.

But don't let that stop you from reading our story and becoming purposeful about your own.

The majority of what we learned came from a few core sources: Dave Ramsey and his personal finance plan; Tony Robbins and his books on money; and Grant Cardone's book on obsession. In some ways these three sources are worlds apart from each other in life experiences and methods, yet I learned valuable, common sense life and money lessons from all of them.

Dave Ramsey showed us simple but effective methods for how to budget, how to pay down debt, how to become millionaires, and how to handle money from a faith-based perspective.

Tony Robbins taught me about taking control of my life and money, and how to invest like the richest men and women in the world (does the name Warren Buffet ring any bells?).

Grant Cardone inspired me to become completely obsessed with my life and to attack my goals with infinite effort (and a workaholic work ethic that people might speak negatively about).

I've read *a lot* of books about money and personal finance. They have all been instructive and motivational. But none of them have felt personal.

I love twelve-step plans. I appreciate a good formula and a kick-butt pep talk. I welcome being called out on my crap and learning how to fix whatever I've broken.

But sometimes I want to read about the hard stuff. The gritty details. I want to know what happened between steps three and four when the plan felt impossible. I want to be told what to do and why to do it, but I also want to know why it will be difficult or what could trip me up and hold me back.

I want to know that someone has been in my shoes and that it didn't destroy them. I want to know about their strengths and success, but I also want to know that sometimes they fail. Or that they doubt their abilities. I want to read about a normal human experience from a...well, a human.

I want to read about the times when they knew that what they were doing was worth it, but it didn't feel worth it at all. I want to know that I'm not the only person who wants to give up and procrastinate and spend too much money on a coffee machine (and let me tell you, I have spent so much money on coffee machines – no regrets!).

I haven't read that book yet. I'm sure it's out there and I hope I find it one day. I hope I find more than one.

So in the meantime, I wrote one.

I don't have studies or statistics to back up what we did and advise. We were asked a lot of questions about what we did and why we did it, and this book is our answer.

We're two normal people putting one foot in front of the other each day, just like you.

But we did this cool thing and we want to tell you about it.

THE RULES (I made these up)

Do NOT compare yourself to us.

> At all, not ever, not once. Don't do it.
>
> Don't compare our debt amount, income, pace we worked at, or any other piece of negativity your brain wants to throw at you.

Do NOT feel ashamed of where you are.

> Whatever headspace you're in right now, chances are we've been there too.
>
> Embarrassment, confusion, anger, fear, denial, or indignation – been there, felt that. *We validate you.*

Stop looking back. You'll have a sore neck for weeks.

> Seriously, the past isn't changing no matter how many times we ruminate on it. Use it when necessary to see how far you've come – but other than that, leave it there. *Especially the regret.* There's no place for that in your present.

Keep an open mind.

> This is difficult because we're all taught that *whatever* we're taught is the most superior information known to man.

But remember: I just cited three people with very different views, and I learned equally valuable information from all of them. And in this same vein...

Think for yourself.

Don't do or not do anything just because we said so. Follow this rule for each piece of information you absorb. Only do what you fully understand and what brings you success that you value.

Accept the reality (and possibility) of setbacks.

They suck, but they don't last.

Celebrate victories.

Every single one.

two tickets to a place to hide, please

"I'm sorry...it won't accept your card."

Now multiply that statement three times for two different debit cards. *What's going on?* Time to call the bank – something is messed up with our debit cards!

Wait, here's a third card; try that. Oh, it worked? It took that one? But...it's attached to the same bank. Different account, though. That's weird.

Phone call to the bank: *Something is wrong with the cards, where's our money, fix it NOW.*

Overdrawn? By HOW much?

How is that possible?

Oh...and overdraft fees...and more *overdraft fees...?*

We went and saw a movie after that. I don't remember what movie, because I was barely able to pay attention. Instead I sat through it feeling warm with shame and embarrassment, thinking up scenarios and explanations that would make this whole ordeal NOT my fault.

But it was totally my fault.

We had two accounts, one his and one mine. We each had a card connected to my account and this was also attached to the savings account. There was money in the savings account, but that night when we tried to buy popcorn and a drink – a mere eight dollar purchase – the checking account was so negatively overdrawn that it's *almost* funny now.

How could that happen, you ask? *Why weren't you paying attention, don't you have jobs, where are your parents young lady, who overdrafts more than three times and doesn't notice it?*

Believe me, I was asking myself the same questions.

Essentially, money was coming out of the account, and when there was no more money in the account it triggered the *super helpful convenient* feature that takes the money from savings to cover (i.e. enable) the purchase.

I say enable because this feature allows the purchase instead of declining the card due to insufficient funds. But each time this happens the account is overdrawn with a fee attached, and the checking account goes further into the negative. (I'll tell you now: the total amount we were in the red for was in the hundreds.)

That was the technical answer to how this happened, but technicalities alone don't cause problems. So how and *why* did this happen?

It happened because I was prideful and cocky about my "ability" to handle money, and because I refused to consider another way of living life financially.

It happened because we were expensing more than was coming in, and we had deluded ourselves into thinking we weren't living paycheck to paycheck. We weren't going hungry or maxing out credit cards or unable to pay our rent, but we certainly weren't making progress to pay off our debt and save money.

I don't even want to admit to this, but I'll fess up to the times I took more student loans than I needed, with plans to use the extra amount for living expenses or purchasing other things.

Yes, you read that correctly: I ended up paying off student loans I didn't have to take out in the first place. Including the interest on them. What a treat.

And we still went to see the movie after this upsetting event.

That should tell you that we were NOT serious about changing our behavior or our lives...not yet, at least.

i'm sort of a know-it-all

Following the overdraft debacle at the movie theater, we agreed something had to change.

But I was SO reluctant to change and adapt. I didn't want to admit that I had messed up and didn't have it all under control.

I'd been making and managing my own money since I was sixteen. My parents taught me how to use a debit card, write in a checkbook, use mobile banking, talk to bankers, take money out of an account, and manage my income and expenses without overspending. Clearly, I knew everything. *(Except, clearly, I didn't know everything.)*

I went to college on my own dime, set up financial aid with an advisor each semester, and was in control of my payment plan, interest fees, FAFSA, financial documentation, taxes, all of it. I was the person friends came to when they had questions about their accounts. I helped more than a few people complete their FAFSA and helped set up details for post-graduation repayment.

I. Was. Fine.

This overdrawn account thing was just a fluke. Something got messed up in the system. A setting in our account had been overlooked.

We made enough money. We paid our bills early, we gave gifts at Christmas, we fixed car repairs, and sometimes we even donated to charity.

Truthfully, these were only facts I spouted out of context.

We didn't make a ton of money. We spent more than we needed to. We fixed car repairs, but dreaded the next one. We wanted to make more money, but didn't actually MAKE more money. We took vacations we shouldn't have taken. (Because we all *deserve* vacations, don't we?) We made only minimum payments on Jason's student loans. We didn't pay any on mine (they weren't "due" yet, after all). We didn't have a substantial savings account. We didn't have a plan.

We were coasting on our tiny piece of good fortune, the most average of average twenty-something people I knew.

When we got married my dad gifted us with his copy of Financial Peace University, Dave Ramsey's program for handling household and personal finances and for learning how to become financially successful.

But I was conceited and brushed it off, saying we'd get to it eventually.

I was *so* busy working and being in school. I was *so* much better than the people who needed that program. I had even started one of his books in college (but stopped reading just a few chapters in). I had my own "system" and I didn't really need anybody else's input. *I did not need help.*

Maybe this money advice stuff was great for some people, but not for me. I just didn't need it and couldn't relate. I'd get to it one day. In the meantime, thanks, but no thanks.

Until that stupid movie theater thing.

Now I would *have* to take a closer look at things. Because the look I was taking wasn't close enough; it was barely a glance and I only saw what I wanted to see.

Where do you start, then? When your mess blows up in your face, you can't cover an eight-dollar expense, your account is deep, dark red, and your ego is so inflated you could make balloon animals from it...then what?

You take the wedding gift, pick up the materials, and swallow allll that sickly sweet pride. That's what I did, at least.

I picked up the program, bought the book I had dismissed in college, downloaded my first ever podcast and decided: This is it. It's this or nothing else. My ways weren't working, so it was time to try ways that are proven to be effective.

Jason had already developed his own way to help control the situation. He started looking at our spending closely. For a short period of time he tracked what came in and what went out: every purchase, each nickel and dime. Every grocery receipt, pizza so many nights a week, library fines (yes, library fines!), Redbox rentals we kept too long...everything. On paper, in red ink and undeniable.

Here's what we found: we weren't doing terribly, but we weren't doing great. We had a lot of potential with our income and expenses. We weren't slaves to our debit cards or our spending patterns and habits. Things didn't have to stay the way they were.

Despite my know-it-all attitude that helped get us into this situation, we could change everything.

the truth about financial success

There is at least a small part in each one of us that wants to be successful. Some of us seek success with more tenacity than others, but for the most part we all want to be fulfilled and happy. And to a lot of us, that's what success looks like. Having what we need (and maybe even all that we want) can contribute to these lifelong goals.

But we are told a lot of things about success and happiness: things we should do or not do, items we need to have, or a certain lifestyle we need to live.

Sometimes it's forgotten that success for me could be different than it is for you. And to be fair, your outlook of success may not have anything to do with money and financial status. Even my own view of it has shifted over the years.

Four years ago if you asked me what being financially successful means, I would have said having a heap of money saved, an even larger heap of money earned, secure investments to live off of, and the lavish vacations to celebrate (and show off) with.

But the time we spent becoming debt-free gave me a new perception of success and happiness. I began to appreciate being successful on another scale (not a "smaller" scale; just another scale).

If you ask me what financial success looks like now, it's being debt-free, saving money for goals and our future, earning the money we need in a way that fulfills us, and knowing that there is more to life than financial progress and a yearly vacation.

Financial success for me is based both on the large, exhilarating goals (paying off $105,000), and the day-to-day decisions and actions needed to make the large goals happen.

The first truth about financial success is that it doesn't have to mean the same thing to every person. The second truth is that each step we take, big or small, contributes to our achievements, and those steps are all successes in and of themselves.

To become debt-free, we had to take small steps. Thinking we were successful only when the debt was cleared would have been a disservice to us and to our efforts.

Success was not just something we were working toward; it was something we were creating. It would not be granted as soon as the debt was paid and our money was ours again; it was something we had to decide to experience every day.

What does financial success mean to you? What does it look and feel like?

Does it look like owning your home? Having a high credit score? Being debt-free and stacking cash to retire early? Does it depend on a certain income or a yearly raise? Do you daydream about flying first class or eating out wherever and whenever you want?

Maybe your financial success has nothing to do with income or spending. Is it found in working whatever job you want regardless of the pay? Giving to every charity that tugs on your heartstrings? What about taking care of aging parents and grandparents, or putting your brilliant niece through college?

And if those types of success seem extravagant and out of your mental league, don't worry. Financial success is also experienced in saving for a new furniture set, washing dishes by hand to cut down on the electric bill, paying rent each month on time or early, or selling items online to fund your next car.

Financial success is whatever you want it to be.

But first you have to think about and decide what that is. Once you do that, you can focus on your money goals and changes.

Choosing what we value as success first is important because making changes with our money is hard. At times it feels like we're never doing "enough." Or we're worried we'll screw it up (again) and fail.

But you'll only fail if you decide that you have.

That night in the movie theater felt like a colossal failure. It was awkward, surprising, and embarrassing. So when we started this process, it was important for us to feel successful with our money. That is what would keep us sprinting toward our goals without being afraid we would trip and fall (and fail).

We decided to value every change and moment of growth as a success. There was truly no victory too small. Each dollar we paid off was success. Every extra hour we worked was a victory. We were successful when we admitted to our financial mistakes, and then learned and tried new ways to handle our money.

The idea of success can feel intimidating. Out of reach. Not meant for us. That's why the third truth about financial success is the most exciting: It *is* meant for you and it is *not* out of reach.

money mindset

Well, that's all well and good, but in a money mess like mine, how does one become financially successful?

Oh, I'm glad you asked.

When I admitted to myself that it was time to make changes, I knew it wouldn't be enough to make money and hope the financial success (and mess) would take care of itself.

First we had to relearn how to handle our money with wisdom. This was part of laying the groundwork for our new behaviors, the behaviors that would build our foundation for financial success.

The two core behaviors we needed to learn and practice were being intentional with our dollars and setting boundaries for our finances. These intentions and boundaries would be seen in our budget, spending, and our focus.

But it wasn't enough to simply learn and then act. Something had to happen in between, and if this didn't happen, the foundation wouldn't be secure.

I had to reexamine, develop, and then practice a healthy money mindset.

Do you feel in control of your money? Or does it seem like money controls you?

Are your thoughts about money flustered and fearful? Do you feel burdened by your finances? Does the word 'finances' make you cringe?

Does handling money freak you out and give you anxiety? Do you worry about the next time you have to put gas in your car?

(I have some good news. Answering any of those questions with honesty is success.)

I know there are a lot of things we have to consider when we think about personal finances: bank accounts, credit and debit cards, credit scores, loans, payments, interest, "money down," savings, budgeting, investing, retirement, and more.

It's overwhelming. (You can breathe out now, because even I hold my breath when reading that list.)

My view of practicing this mindset involves practicality and application.

I love thinking about money as energy and as an element that's abundant in my life, and I believe that positive thoughts and beliefs help us create our reality. But to me, a healthy money mindset is similar to knowledge: in most situations, it is nothing without action. So let's *do* something about this.

The first step to being in control and creating a healthy money mindset is to look at your situation honestly. So take a step back from all of those heavy considerations I just listed and clear your head from the panicked thoughts and looming dollar signs.

The second step is to start looking at your money in its most basic form: the amount that comes into your possession (what you earn or are gifted) and the amount that leaves your possession (through spending, bills, or otherwise). Become familiar with these two numbers and (for now) forget the rest. You can get to that later. It's important to start here.

(More good news: Knowing what comes in and what goes out of your bank accounts, and hopefully one day not being ashamed of either number, is success.)

When we take control of our money, we take control of our entire lives. It doesn't matter if you make $20,000 a year or $200,000 a year. If you are in control of the money coming in and going out, no matter the amount, you are financially successful.

Learning to talk and think about money is freeing and empowering. Checking your bank account with certainty you won't be seeing red and without fear of the balance are positive goals to work toward. Don't be afraid of your money. You made it, after all; you get to decide what to do with it. (This is a very good and powerful thing!)

I love talking about money (yours, mine, or anyone else's). Making money, saving money, budgeting, spending, and investing money. I know a lot of people do not feel this way and I respect their feelings. (And if you are one of these people, it's important that you know it doesn't have to be this way.)

But maybe you're like me. Maybe you think you have a solid money mindset and you don't need to examine or change it to achieve financial success.

I never feared handling money. I never feared not having "enough." I always thought I had a good money mindset because I thought personal finances were easy and exciting. I made money, I paid bills, I spent what I wanted to, and life was good. I thought the success would take care of itself.

But I was not immune to making poor financial decisions. I liked dealing with my money and I enjoyed the intricate topics of economics, but in my pride I forgot to look at my money in a simple way.

In fact, I forgot to look at it at all. Instead, I tried to think and learn about everything else at the same time, and I lost focus on the most important numbers right in front of me: what came in and what went out.

During my undergraduate years and semesters in graduate programs, somewhere along the way I stopped paying attention to the reality of taking on so many student loans (my debt mess). I didn't want to judge myself for the debt, but I also failed to look at the situation honestly.

After the wake-up call at the movie theater, I understood why personal finances could freak someone out. After all, I thought I knew what I was doing, and look at what I got myself into!

Looking at my student loan balance was now terrifying. These numbers were not fictional symbols and there were a lot of zeroes. This translated into cold hard cash I would have to earn and part with. This number was now a barrier to my future, a limitation I put into place without realizing it.

And my harsh reality check was this: now that I was looking at them again, I saw that the numbers coming in and going out were not going to take care of this debt.

I had become so mentally removed from the truth of my financial situation. Before this point, the student loans were just numbers I would have to take care of One Day. The debt was normal, acceptable, and expected. *And it was growing.*

My so-called healthy money mindset backfired. It became bleak and anxious.

I get it now, I remember thinking. I know why people can't bear to look at their reality and their mess.

I understand how it feels to be deep into the hole. The ground feels like sinking sand, the sides are caving in, and the footholds are slipping away. The sky is disappearing, sounds are muffled, and it's so hard to breathe.

"Just climb out!" everyone is saying, but they don't understand. Can't they see how far down you are?

"Just reach up and grab my hand!" But everything is dark and you are plummeting deeper and deeper.

In this isolated, fearful mindset, every life task begins to feel like that hole. Going to work feels pointless because that part of life feels as if it's out of our hands. Parting with money is difficult, but somehow impulse shopping is still so easy (because it feels good, better than anything else). Procrastination looks appealing despite its slow suffocation. *"I'll deal with it tomorrow. It might take care of itself."*

My isolation and fear joined forces with complacency. I then understood that each time I had taken on more loans without confronting the consequences, I was justifying this means to an end. (And, secretly, I couldn't see another way out, so I told myself that my situation was different and excusable.)

Before this confrontation with reality, I had crafted a narrative to tell myself, a story to push down my fear and cover my problems.

I'm still in school, I'm figuring out my life, I'm working full-time, we are getting there...We don't have a car payment or credit cards or a mortgage; we aren't in the red or buying expensive things, and we even pay with cash sometimes...

Yes, these were facts, but I was abusing them and fitting them to tell myself a more desirable story. I wanted to support my so-called money mindset.

But once I looked at our situation honestly, I saw the need to regain control. I didn't want to stay in this negative and anxious mindset. And I also didn't want to return to a mindset built on pride and complacent delusions.

I adopted a healthy money mindset by owning my mess and facing the consequences. I accepted reality and allowed myself to crave growth and change.

But the mindset alone wasn't enough. It was a necessary starting point, but it alone wouldn't create the end results we wanted.

If you think you have a good money mindset but you're in a similar situation, it's time to reexamine.

Take step one and look at your situation honestly, and then take step two and focus on your money in its most basic form. Then work your way to owning the mess, facing the consequences, accepting reality, and craving growth and change.

I loved thinking and talking about money, but it was time to do much more than think and talk. It was time to lay groundwork, build a foundation, and take action.

time to cut the cord and get up from the chair

Spending so much time in one place and one frame of mind can lead to getting very, very comfortable. A little too comfortable, if it keeps us from recognizing the need for change and growth.

This comfort leads to complacency and the complacency shimmers into apathy; soon we're debilitated, unable to get up from the overstuffed recliner that fits to our mold perfectly.

The recliner chair I sat in for too long was school: "getting an education." I went from one degree to the next, hoping to satisfy a void in me that would equal meaning and purpose, one I was sure could be filled with the "right" career path.

Education is great. Lifelong learning is something to aspire to.

Seventy thousand dollars in student loan debt is NOT.

Did you read that correctly? Clearly my eyes glimpsed over it too many times as I racked up loan after loan.

SEVENTY. THOUSAND. DOLLARS.

At that point in my life, outside of working in high school, in total I'd barely *made* over seventy thousand dollars. Let alone racking it up in loans I would have to repay? My heart starts beating faster just thinking about it, and I don't even owe it anymore!

I had patted myself on the back for graduating with my degree with less than forty-five thousand dollars in loans. I'd paid at least ten thousand dollars out of pocket each year, which felt like an achievement at the time.

But then I enrolled in graduate programs, took on another twenty thousand dollars of debt, and kept back patting because I would have a Master's degree. That felt so good to think, to say.

It made the debt feel worth it – for half a minute.

By the time I decided the second graduate program wasn't the right one, I was close to seventy thousand dollars (interest included) in debt, and the movie theater ordeal had already happened.

I was torn between feeling the urgent need to find a new career path and program to try, and the knowledge that our money situation was precarious and we needed to overhaul our personal finances.

But I was deep in that hole. There was too much going on and I didn't want to look at my mess.

My mindset was still dark and I felt betrayed. I felt betrayed by my assumptions that finding the right career would solve my problems and complete my life, and then having it backfire into a glorious volcano of rejection in my face. No degree usage. No career. No self-worth funded by a decent income. Just a flamethrower shot into my plans, leaving behind a white-hot pile of student loans and shame.

But I knew it was time to cut the cord. I couldn't justify adding more to the ever-growing number. I wasn't where I wanted to be in life, but if I wasn't careful I'd spend so much time striving that I'd never get there either way. Plus, by the time I figured anything out we'd have so much debt it wouldn't matter.

During this bout of inner turmoil, we had started paying Jason's student loans and would soon have to start payments on mine. Being enrolled in school meant I could keep deferring the repayment and stay in a perpetual grace period.

But this period was no longer one of grace. It was now denial, complacency, fear, and, frankly, absurdity. And we knew that we'd both have to see this for any changes to be effective. We had to do it together.

When I told Jason I couldn't continue with more school paid for by loans, he understood why and didn't question this realization. We decided I would take the coming semester off and pay with cash for the next program when I found it.

In the meantime, it was time to get serious and get to work. It was time to get up from that chair.

dear me, I forgive you

I met one of my closest friends in college. Within the first two weeks of classes we were introduced through a series of random events and decided we were going to be best friends. That was nine years ago, and even from miles away our friendship only gets better each year.

Before this friendship, my other friendships were handed to me through school classmates, church groups, and family friends. I never had to seek out new people or do much work in the way of maintaining the relationships.

This was my first adult friendship that taught me lessons about making friendships and relationships work. Before, I'd shied away from confrontational conversations, opposing opinions, disagreements, or doing and saying anything that would make me not part of the group. I didn't know that people could have arguments or fights and still be friends afterwards.

But this new friend was not shy about her opinions, did not fuss about making waves, did not mind disagreements and arguments, and fully expected me to feel the same way in our friendship.

We had our first gut-wrenching fight our freshman year. My initial reactions were to pull away and assume the friendship was over. I didn't know we could work out the problems and forgive and move on. I didn't know we could agree to disagree and still respect and love each other just as much, if not more.

I didn't know that building our relationship on a foundation of respect and forgiveness would make us stronger as people and as friends.

What's the point of this story?

So I made a friend and learned obvious life lessons and now things are great. So what? What does that have to do with getting out of debt?

The foundation of respect and forgiveness I learned is what has everything to do with getting out of debt.

I applied for student loans because I didn't allow myself to believe or learn that there was another way to pay for college.

I didn't consider going to community college, taking a year off to save, taking classes on a slower-paced schedule, or commuting for all four years instead of only the last one. I berated myself for not having higher SAT scores, for not applying to more scholarships, and for not saving more money in high school.

I came into this new financial situation with the burden of my negativity and then I did nothing but add to it.

I took on more student loans for graduate school because I criticized myself for not selecting a better major for my undergraduate and for not changing my major when I had the opportunity. I took this burden of shame and, once again, I only added to it.

And each time I signed up for another loan, I told myself that this was okay, because student debt was normalized and tolerable.

I wasted a lot of time feeling sorry for myself and spent a lot of time apologizing to and seeking forgiveness from everyone for the mess I had created.

Everyone but myself.

I never apologized to present Me for the decisions past Me made, the ones that present Me would now have to deal with. Worse than that, I had never forgiven past Me for making those decisions.

Before I started making changes to my habits and money mindset, I had to have a hard conversation with myself that may seem silly, but was necessary for action and growth.

Dear me, I forgive you. I know you did what you thought was best. I know you did certain things because they were the only things you knew to do. It's not completely your fault that you didn't know any better or different.

It's not your fault you were scared of change and chose a school situation that was comfortable. I think it's great that you took on this challenge and burden of putting yourself through college, and I think it's cool that you have a degree (even if we don't use it).

I forgive you for not saving as much money in high school. I forgive you for not taking the SAT again. I forgive you for totaling our car freshman year and having to pay cash for another one. I forgive you for relationship choices that cost a lot of time and money.

I forgive you for spending money on things we didn't need, and I forgive you for that time you forgot to pay the school bill and owed a late fee and interest fee almost as much as the bill itself. And for that time you forgot to return your rented books for the semester and had to pay the buy-out fees. I know that sucked; those books were useless.

I forgive you for jumping into graduate programs. I know it was hard to feel purposeless and inferior to the people around you who were doing important things with their degrees. I forgive you for not working more and for taking out more loans to pay for household expenses.

But also, I respect you. You got us this far, and without you I wouldn't know how to take this next step.

Thank you for all the good choices you made. They outnumber the bad ones a million to one. Thank you for not giving up. Thank you for learning everything I needed to know, even though at times I seem ungrateful for it.

Thank you for this opportunity to change my life and do something amazing.

You have to forgive yourself.

Shame and embarrassment and finger pointing will not take you into the money mindset you need to handle your personal finances and make the powerful changes you need to make.

I know it royally SUCKS to look back and see where you went wrong. I know it is frustrating as crap to learn information that had you known it then, could have saved you from this discomfort and the challenge that's ahead. I know it's tempting to feel that you got gypped and this struggle isn't fair.

Maybe you are like me and you only did what you knew to do, and now it feels like it backfired. And maybe you are also like me and you know you could have made better choices that you knew were better at the time.

Either way, forgiveness doesn't just make these changes and this growth easier. It also makes it possible.

we forgive, but never forget

The facts and events below look a lot like regrets, but we do our best not to view them in that way anymore. Instead, we try to see them as learning experiences (just very expensive ones).

Acknowledging them and forgiving ourselves for them is how we moved forward and adopted our new money mindsets.

We accept responsibility for all of these decisions, as uninformed and rushed as they were.

Rushing and forcing life has cost us both time and money.

$ I could have gone to college without going into debt or at least graduated with half the amount of student loans.

$ I picked my college based on the campus aesthetics, proximity to my family, and the fact that a close friend from high school was attending.

$ I chose my degree out of fear and uncertainty and wish I had picked something else.

$ I could have saved us an additional twenty thousand dollars in loans if I hadn't enrolled in two different graduate programs (neither of which I finished, by the way...).

$ I could have worked more when I graduated college, instead of starting the graduate degrees (did I mention I didn't finish them?).

$ We paid cash for a certificate program I completed but will not be using (sensing a theme here...).

$ Jason attended a traditional four-year college because 'that's what people do.' He did not understand the full implications of taking on loans, and took them because 'that's what people do.'

$ He only completed two years of college because he did not choose a major that suited him for the future.

$ He did not have a job during college when he admits he 100% had the time to.

$ He spent his savings account as if it was a trust fund (except, trust funds rarely run out...).

Take the time to acknowledge where you are with your personal finances and what brought you to this point. It's good to identify patterns and habits, like I did when I saw that I put my finances into a scary place for the sake of trying different degrees. I recognized this as a pattern and habit I needed to change.

Damaging patterns can show up in different forms: spending habits, impulse shopping, using a new credit card before paying off an old one, or rolling upside-down car debt into another financing plan. The ways we can disrupt our financial success are endless.

Do something concrete with this information: write it out and don't hold back. Confront the past and the truth.

Then, forgive yourself, and be inspired to learn from these mistakes and rewrite the rest of your story.

why debt-free? and why the rush?

Technically speaking, a debt in the way we often think of it is just another payment. Like the payment we make for Internet, our car insurance, or our Hulu account. Yes, there's a balance that's owed, but isn't it still the same as the other payments we make?

I grappled with this question while I was in college. Sometimes I felt bad for the student loans because the feeling, though normalized, was claustrophobic. But since then I have identified an important distinction between the two types of payments.

If I wanted to stop making payments on my Hulu or Netflix accounts, I would lose the subscription service. But I wouldn't owe the company any more money, and I wouldn't have to pay this payment ever again unless I wanted to restart the subscription plan.

This is not the case with a student loan payment or a payment on other consumer debt. Making a monthly payment might lower the loan amount, but stopping the payments doesn't cancel out the loan balance.

(Wouldn't this whole thing be so much easier if it did? *'Hey, yeah, I think I'm good with the payments I've made, so I'm just going to cut out now and that's cool, right?'*)

That's why a loan payment is not just a payment. It is debt. It is money borrowed that has to be paid back. And most of the time the debt comes with interest (best part!) and the payment pays the interest first (worst part!). Theoretically, you could pay the same payment on the same loan over and over again and hardly lower the loan balance because you're mostly repaying the interest (sad part).

The first reason we wanted to become debt-free was to get rid of the claustrophobic feelings. I didn't like the feeling of owing this large sum of money. I didn't like the sky-is-falling scenarios it put into my head: What if we lose our incomes or have a sudden emergency and can't pay the payments and the interest just keeps adding to the balance? What if we want to buy a house and the debt ratio counts against us (hint: it might) and limits the amount we can get for a mortgage?

The second reason was to get rid of the interest adding up. Repaying money that I didn't borrow or use felt...stupid. And annoying. I would be glad to be rid of those feelings.

The third reason we wanted to become debt-free was because we wanted our income back. Our total loan payment was eight hundred dollars a month, and that was without paying extra to head off the interest accruing. We would have rather kept that money and used it for something that we enjoyed, like...literally anything else.

These top three reasons are also why we wanted to do this as fast and as soon as possible.

I suppose we could have taken our time and done other things with our income while steadily paying the loans. But we would still feel claustrophobic, I would still fear the sky falling, and we wouldn't feel that our income was truly ours.

Owing debt from money we borrowed made us feel like our income was borrowed, too. If we took care of it as fast as possible, we would never have to deal with any of those feelings and worries again.

A fourth reason we wanted to become debt-free, and as quickly as possible, was because when we realized we needed to change how we handled our money, we wanted to do more than fill out a budget form and change the investment strategy for retirement.

We wanted to do something epic that would prove to ourselves that we took this seriously and we were willing to do anything to create financial security and success.

$1,000 emergency fund

While I was still enrolled in school, the first major task we did was start the program my dad had given us. We began with the audio recordings of the then-version of Financial Peace University.

At first I was skeptical and rudely critical. Was this going to be like a sermon with some well-placed punch lines? Would I have to fill out the workbook to learn the information? Would the information even be useful? Would it be relevant to me?

I'm glad that I'm not the cynic I used to be, but to this day I'm surprised I gave the program a chance at all.

It was a complete mental renovation. We learned so much from these recordings. Some of it is cheesy at times, but the common sense was surprising and legitimate. We were learning information we'd never learned before. The financial status quo of society was being challenged. It was invigorating and exciting.

But most importantly, *we began to feel hope.*

We felt confident that we could do this. Our entire future changed as we listened to this program. We were in control again and WE would create our lives. WE would happen to our future and time, instead of feeling life was happening to us.

Now armed with this knowledge and a plan, I wasn't so afraid of our student loans. I was ready to face them head-on, fully grounded in this new reality.

The program is broken down into seven "baby steps." To get out of debt, we followed the first two.

The first step in the plan is to save one thousand dollars and to set it somewhere it won't be touched unless in the case of an emergency (pizza deliveries, Netflix price increases, and another pair of shoes are not emergencies). Doesn't matter how you save or acquire it, just do it and do it fast.

We were prepared to immediately cut down on spending, sell items we didn't need, and take on extra working hours. Instead we mentally high-fived each other because we already had this money set aside.

Step one was completed. It felt so good to accomplish something.

When we don't plan for emergencies or anticipate unexpected costs and needs, life happens chaotically and we lose our grip on what's going on with our money.

We borrow money, rely on credit cards, sign up for financing and payment plans, and operate like an upset child who just had an ice cream cone knocked from her hand: drama, drama, drama. Step onto this ride too many times and you'll never get off.

If we never prepare for the problems, everything will be a problem.

Twenty dollars isn't a big deal, but when payday isn't until Friday and the gas tank is empty and the phone bill is due and the lights are flickering in the apartment, twenty dollars is suddenly a big deal.

It's easy to get caught up in small regrets and reprimand ourselves for innocent expenses: 'Shouldn't have bought that pizza three weeks ago...should have waited for that pair of jeans I needed to replace...should have borrowed from the library instead of Redbox...'

But having a healthy money mindset is about more than dealing with money stressors by upending the couch cushions to look for spare change. It's about learning to prevent these stressors completely and far before the electricity cuts out.

I know amounts of money can be relative, but quibbling over these smaller purchases is crazy. Twenty dollars should never be our problem. Two hundred dollars should never be a problem.

Instead, what if we prepared for the problems and had a plan in place to make sure these issues were never issues at all? What if instead of becoming drama queens about every life event, we were calm and steady and held a royal flush, ready to throw it down at a moment's need?

That's what setting aside the one thousand dollars is to me: heading off problems and happening to life before it can happen to me.

"What's a thousand bucks going to do in a 'real' emergency?" (A question I've been asked many times, and one I even wondered myself.)

Well, for one, it could buy me a new prescription for my glasses so I could see what was really going on here. It's not really about the thousand dollars. It's about being prepared for the small stuff that throws us off and gets in the way of our financial success and the potential for calm, drama-free living.

One thousand dollars can, for instance, pay for the immediate emergency of a car broken down on the side of the road, four hours from your house and with only rental cars in sight...

We were driving to West Virginia for a friend's wedding that I was in.

We finished listening to the recordings that summer, had our one thousand dollars in the bank, and I was taking my break from school. We were in the process of setting aside money for a new car and also saving cash for my next schooling program. We still hadn't started paying my loans but we were developing our new money mindsets about the process and the reality we were facing.

These were our first small victories. (In some ways, I now believe they were the most important ones.)

My own mindset had not changed overnight. I was still cocky about handling money, and still reluctant to commit fully to the plan, to any plan. I guess I needed a 'Gotcha!' moment to humble my attitude and inspire more commitment and action.

The cord was cut, I was up off the chair, but I hadn't really *moved* yet.

The wedding was a little over four hours away from our house. We were staying in town for a few nights and had paid for the hotel, my dress, and other related expenses with ease.

But about an hour from the destination I felt the car slowing down no matter how hard I pressed on the gas or revved the engine. *Not again.* We'd had similar car troubles in the past, but usually close to home and issues we could fix inexpensively.

I pulled over to the side of the road and Jason checked the car. It was clear we were stuck: this car wasn't getting us to the wedding. We called for a tow that would take us into the nearest town and to a car rental. We had to pack all our stuff into the tow truck and then move it again into the car rental building while we waited for a vehicle. *Classy.*

The cheapest car they had available was that years' model of a Toyota Camry (as in, not cheap at all). It was *huge*, with bells and whistles Jason's 2001 Elantra didn't even have technology for. It was almost five hundred dollars for the days we needed it, including the trip home.

Remember what I said about two hundred dollars and it shouldn't be a big deal? Double that number and add some, and I will *still* say it shouldn't be a big deal. A five hundred dollar emergency shouldn't make my chest constrict, my fists clench with fearful frustration, or my brain shout that the sky is falling.

And that day, it didn't. Would you like to know why?

We had *the one thousand dollar emergency fund.* We didn't have to skip the wedding, fight temptation to use a credit card (that we didn't and don't have, but imagine if we did), or ask to borrow the money from our friends or from my dad when he came and towed the car home.

"What's a thousand bucks going to do in a 'real emergency'?"

I had my answer. It saved our trip to that wedding. It turned this potentially stressful problem and emergency into a mere inconvenience.

I wasn't a fan of having to rent an expensive car, but after that initial moment of annoyance the situation didn't faze me. We prepared for life, and when life happened we were ready.

For the first time, we could feel it: financial success was amazing.

Since that incident we've used the emergency fund only a handful of times. And every time we've replenished it as soon as possible.

Generally, we use our income and cash flow to spot us for unexpected inconveniences, but having that extra padding is part of the difference between living and paying off debt with mental security, or watching the bank accounts with heart palpitations and fear.

We've used the fund for another large car repair; to help fund Jason's replacement car; a surgery for our cat; and a few other miscellaneous "emergencies" that I barely remember because we didn't experience them as pressing emergencies. Instead they were only annoying inconveniences.

But why one thousand dollars? Why not two, three, five? Or why not five hundred dollars?

The plan recommended one thousand because with the average household income this seems to be a number that would cover almost any major emergency.

Clearly, five hundred wouldn't have been enough for our wedding trip. It would have just barely covered the car but depleted the fund entirely. What if something else went wrong on the trip? But we didn't have to worry about that because the amount we had was sufficient.

If you feel you need more than a thousand, do two thousand. Heck, do three or five thousand. But don't get caught up on the number. At first I did, and then I reminded myself: on most days before this I didn't even have a thousand dollars to begin with, so who was I to argue we would need more?

I also reminded myself that these changes and this process would require small steps first. Proving we could take these steps and make these smaller changes (and handle this smaller amount of money) would prepare us for bigger changes and for handling larger amounts of money.

pay off all debt

This is probably why you're reading this book. I hope you didn't open it with expectations of money secrets or tips and tricks, like saving every five dollar bill you get or investing your change, or saving a dollar a day for a year. I do believe in small changes leading to success, but this process would require massive action.

This step is very straightforward and took us two-and-a-half-years. Pay off all debt as fast as humanly possible.

That's it.

There's no secret. No scam. No magic tricks.

Bring as much money as possible in and pay it allll back out until you're done, until you're DEBT-FREE.

budget: another four-letter word

You're upset now, aren't you? I threw in the B-word. I got technical less than halfway in to the story. Well, I never said it was easy! I never said it would be a good time!

But it's possible and it's worth it, and we had to work hard and smart to make it happen.

"I hate budgeting."

"I don't *do* budgeting."

"Budgeting is boring."

"I don't like feeling restricted."

"*I* don't need a budget."

"Can't I just....do it without one?"

These are things people say to me in the middle of recounting how we paid off our loans. And at first I wanted to say these things, too.

Despite my positivity toward talking about and handling money, I didn't want it to ever feel difficult or let it take up too much of my time and mental energy. My plan for handling income was loose and had no solid structure. The concept of a budget was important and I knew it was fundamental, but I didn't want to put too much effort into it.

Does anybody else ever feel like this with life fundamentals? Things we know are good for us but we wish we could be above and do without? Like eating all our vegetables and drinking the right amount of water...we know we should, we know it's for our benefit, but some days...ugh. Can't we skip it? Don't we have enough to do?

That was how I felt about a detailed budget that I held myself accountable to. Ugh.

I think my true resistance to budgeting came from my belief that having a budget meant you weren't smart with money, or that you didn't know what to do with it without losing it all. I only heard the word associated with negative emotions and not having enough.

I didn't think that wealthy people needed a budget or that people with enough money had to plan their spending. Budgeting was connected with telling myself no and only concerned the annoying boring expenses like bills and gas and insurance plans.

I didn't consider that to become wealthy there might have been a budget involved. And that a budget could be used to tell myself yes *and* no, and that controlling my money wouldn't be negative at all. I didn't realize that a budget could be used to plan *all* of my spending, including the fun stuff.

Admittedly, I also didn't want to have to care too much about it. I wanted to remain attached to my illusion that I had a sufficient income and that putting more effort into creating and managing a budget wouldn't change that. I always thought that what I was doing was enough. Caring too much would show me that I was wrong.

It's also possible I didn't want to confront my low pay that wouldn't accomplish our money goals. And maybe I didn't want to feel like I couldn't do whatever I wanted with my own money.

A budget made me feel like I needed help and implied that I couldn't do it all by myself. And remember: I thought I knew everything. *I. Was. Fine.*

It's obvious that I had a lot of thoughts and feelings about it that held me back and influenced my mindset.

But listen: I don't like doing laundry. I don't like driving far distances. I don't always like cooking or grocery shopping or forking over thirty-seven dollars for car registration. I want to be above these things and do without.

That has yet to mean I get a free pass on doing these things. Frankly, I'm better for doing them. Being a productive adult is a good thing, even when it requires mundane tasks and time I'd rather spend elsewhere.

You know what I also don't like? Being broke. Having an overdrawn checking account. Second-guessing purchases made or bills being paid. Stressing about life decisions because of my finances. Not being able to buy the quality of food and personal products I prefer. Feeling tempted to skimp on a tip.

I had to get over my thoughts and feelings about a structured, detailed budget and decide what was more important: financial progress and success, or another embarrassing moment at the movie theater? Freedom and security with our money and my mindset, or complacent pride and anxiety?

If you think a budget is the worst thing ever, you're probably overcomplicating it or lacking structure. I don't want to say there is a right or wrong way to budget, but failing to plan or overcomplicating any financial process does not feel good or work out in the long term. You already have a lot going on. The last thing you need is budget stress.

If you're getting hung up on the word Budget, change the word. Pick a phrase that you prefer. Your personal finances are a powerful part of your life, good or bad. Embrace them, befriend them, work on them, and control them.

Don't let your feelings about a word or concept command your future. Call it your "money plan," your "monthly money goals," your "In and Out fund," whatever makes you feel in charge of your money.

You have to know what comes in, and you have to know *and control* what goes out.

Don't check your bank account with the mindset of not knowing what's going to be there. The account has your name on it. You own what's in it. You don't look in your own fridge and expect to see more or less than any of the food you've bought and eaten, do you?

And why do we tend to spend so much time at work (work we might not enjoy or prefer) and then not decide what happens to the money we earned, the very *reason* we're there in the first place?

This realization was awkward for me to acknowledge, but once I did I couldn't escape it. I spent a lot of time and energy at work, hustling for the almighty dollar. But then, when I got that dollar, sometimes I threw it away as if it meant nothing to me. Why would I work so hard for something I didn't seem to care about? Why would I work multiple jobs for money I didn't want to have a say over?

Does this seem absolutely crazy to you? It did and still does to me. If for no other financial reason, create and follow a budget because of this realization.

And because you deserve it.

You earned this money and you deserve to tell it where to go or where to stay. You traded your time and energy and you should have a say with what happens to the money you made from it.

A budget (or whatever you call it) is your way to say what happens. It joins forces with your healthy money mindset and your small emergency fund and supports your drama-free living.

It's the gift you give yourself when you get to sit at home with your feet propped up and you have complete control over your hard-earned income.

Keep your money matters simple, but structured and effective.

If you describe your budgeting plan to someone and their eyes glaze over, rework the plan until instead their eyes brighten at the logic and simplicity. When I first learned a new budgeting method, I tried to do it my own way for a few months, but it was not the logical simplicity it could and should have been.

When explaining the process to someone over text message, the longer the paragraph got, the more I realized how complicated it was. They just didn't get it. And no wonder. (Now I think back and am not sure if I got it, either.)

Start with a budget and strategy that you understand and value.

(Side bar: There are a lot of great budgeting methods. I'm sure that with time and effort, they all work. I've also seen that many of them have similar structures and overlapping principles. Because of this, it's fair to say that no method is better than another.

Will one method be better and more effective *for you*? Probably. When you find that method, stick to it, and only change it if *you* feel you need to. If you spend any time in the money or budgeting space online, you'll see a lot of variations and methods and they will all claim they are the best budget. Because they all work.

Here's my two cents. The best method is the one that builds the foundation that puts you in control of your money. This control leads to clear intentions, focus, and accountability. A set-it-and-forget-it budget will not build this foundation.

Don't get caught up in which method or person has the prettiest printables or the nicest wallet and budget binder. In the beginning, do your budget method as simply and cheaply as possible. You don't need to spend money to do this. Your budget is about your mindset and your behavior.)

I learned how to do the zero-based budgeting method. I don't even think of it as a "method" because to me it's common sense. And again, this is not secret magic.

I do mine with pen and paper because I like seeing the numbers in a physical form in front of me. There are apps that do this same process, or also connect to bank accounts and track everything for you; but by now you know – I like doing things myself. I get a rush from the feeling of purpose and control.

On paper, I draw two columns. The column on the left says INCOME and the column on the right says EXPENSES. The basic goal is for what I bring in (income) minus what I spend out (expenses) to equal zero.

This does NOT mean I am spending my entire income. It means I am deciding and stating where every single dollar goes. This is different from tracking my spending, a process that usually happens only after the money is spent. This is deciding my spending *before* it happens.

First I write down our projected incomes. I say projected because our income is not a set amount. We work overtime or different schedules each week and the numbers fluctuate.

If this is the same for you and you get nervous about overestimating your income, pick a base number to use. For example, we always made at least a certain amount before overtime or extra side hustle. When I started this process I used that number under the Income column. It gave me security and certainty that we wouldn't "spend" more than what came in.

I write our expenses in the second column. I start with the monthly bills or payments that have exact amounts. Sometimes I also write them in the order they are paid throughout the month.

These payments include rent, Internet, phone plans, entertainment subscriptions, life insurance, car insurance, and charitable giving. Electric changes monthly, but I can estimate this or use a base number. (If I want be more detailed, I can log into my electric account online and monitor the amount throughout the month.) We also budget in gas and grocery, and though these numbers change monthly I can pick a base amount I know we won't go over.

At first I wasn't sure how much we were spending on food eaten out, food for our home, and gas. I also wasn't sure how much miscellaneous spending we did. I didn't like the feeling of not knowing, especially when I confronted myself about working hard and not working even harder to handle our money.

Before I made our first intentional and thorough budget, I printed our bank account records for the month before and highlighted certain areas of spending. I also looked at the monthly payment items to be sure they were all accounted for in the budget. (I found I had looked over a few subscriptions and realized I was paying for a gym I no longer went to.) I saw what we were spending for gas, groceries, and meals out, and identified spending patterns.

This process showed me a clearer picture of our money decisions and habits. It also made me aware of areas we could consider changing and services we could cancel.

After a few months of successful and confident budgeting, I printed the bank records again and repeated the process. I had kept every month's budget and that first set of bank records and was able to compare them to our current habits.

The new picture looked a lot better.

The plan we followed recommended doing a new budget for every single month before the month starts. This is because each month is different. We have holidays, birthdays, dinners, social outings and more that changes monthly. We should prepare for these and "budget" them in. If you don't know the exact amount these will be, set an amount you will NOT pay more than.

Remember, this is your money: you decide what to do with it. This is both your privilege and your right.

If you want to spend forty for a gift, spend forty for a gift. If you want to spend sixty on a dinner, spend sixty (tip included). But plan for it and do it purposefully. And when you set an amount, stick to it! Accidents and mistakes with the budget can happen, but they're less likely to if we plan properly and commit to those plans.

(Just in case you're wondering: If the thought of budgeting for the entire month feels overwhelming, don't do it for the entire month. Still write down your projected and planned expenses for the month, but manage the income and payment part in smaller increments. You can do this by individual paycheck (if you have multiple jobs or household incomes) or by pay period (weekly, biweekly, or monthly).

Plan out how you will spend each paycheck before or as soon as it hits your account, and focus on that smaller period of time in your budget. Also, don't be afraid to change your expenses or details as time passes and paychecks come in. Sometimes life happens unexpectedly; that's okay! You can handle it. *You can do this*.)

Once I list the expenses, I list what I would do with extra money after the expenses are covered. This is where the monthly extras or items we are intentionally saving for will be "paid for." This is also where the debt comes into play in the budget. All extra income left over from our expenses went to the debt. Any extra income not accounted for in the Income column went to it as well.

To keep myself accountable with budgeting extra income, for each month I wrote the actual income amount once our paychecks came in and made sure that extra money was going to the debt. If our base was $1,500 for the week and we earned $2,000, I made a note of the difference and extra income on the budget and noted that the extra $500 went to the loans.

To help with self-control and seeing the numbers more clearly, we also decided to open a second checking account that was attached to our main one. This account would function as a savings account. (This already sounds complicated but keep reading because I promise it's not.)

Our emergency fund sits in this account and each time we had money in checking that would be designated for a loan payment, I moved it into the second checking ("savings") account and made the payment from there.

Separating the accounts and the money creates a boundary in my mind.

Once that money is moved into the second checking account, it's as if it has already been "spent," and I am unlikely to move it back into the other account unless there is an emergency. I did this with the loans, rent, and other large sums that came out of the account. I still do it with rent and items we are saving for. Then I can focus on the first checking account and manage the budget from there.

Setting boundaries for myself has been very healthy. Sometimes boundaries sound like restrictions: "I can't do this, can't have that."

But we are humans and we are not perfect. I had set important goals and was dedicated to our mission, but that did not mean I was suddenly flawless at saving money or not spending more than I should have.

We all need boundaries.

Sometimes we need self-imposed limitations.

I needed to make it easier for myself not to spend money and to set money aside for the debt.

Creating boundaries made this process doable and nearly painless. If the money was in a specific account, it had a specific purpose. If I moved it there with an intention, I was more likely to respect those intentions.

It sounds completely oxymoronic, but setting boundaries gave me freedom. I didn't have to think so hard about spending or not spending. I didn't have to check my bank account before every single purchase and do mental math to figure out what amount was going to be taken out or what amount could be spent (and I definitely didn't want to think about what amount would be left).

Setting boundaries helped me become trustworthy to myself. I trusted that I was doing smart things with our money. I trusted our process and our behavior.

I enjoyed the process, but I didn't agonize over the budget. We were fortunate to have a larger income to expenses ratio and we were never unable to pay our bills, budget extra spending, and put a significant amount to the debt.

I have also developed a stronger sense of accountability within myself, and because our purpose and money intentions are clear I don't worry we will overspend or spend mindlessly.

If this is not the case for you, if you need more detail, accountability, or have a lower income to expenses ratio, be detailed with your budget. Put time and effort into it. Set clear amounts you will allow yourself to spend and only allow that amount in your account or pocket. Track what you spend if that helps you maintain control.

Decide what purpose your money will serve. Set your boundaries. Be intentional with your dollars. Learn to trust yourself.

Then, experience mental and financial freedom.

team us (and team you)

I say "we" a lot, because I'm married and I'm part of a team: a two-person team. Two-person teams aren't part of many popular sports, but when you're married and wanting to function as a healthy couple, that two-person team is the most important one you'll ever play on.

I know that every married couple is different in how they function and live. I can only speak to the one I'm part of.

I chose to be with someone I could trust with our money and financial future. We both wanted our finances to be shared completely and to be combined into one pile of "Married Money."

When we said I Do, we mentally said more than the traditional vows. We said I Do take on your debt as my own debt; I Do plan to combine my income with your income; I Do intend to handle our money as a team and with your input; and I Don't want to do this alone.

I separated the loans into "Jason's student loans" and "Monica's student loans" for the purpose of deciding how and when we would pay each amount, but not once did either of us think, "He or she is responsible for their part and I'm only responsible for mine." It all became one number, and together we took on the burden of getting rid of it.

We did everything together during this process. We agreed on large spending decisions, approved certain parts of the budget, lamented our difficulties and struggles, and celebrated the victories.

I never felt that I was alone or that it was all on me to make this happen. I did handle most of the budgeting and payments, but this was only because I loved doing it, *not* because Jason didn't want to.

We each got to play to our strengths (I hyped myself up and he calmed me down) and that is how we won as a team.

If you're married, I obviously don't know what your situation is. I don't know if you have an unsupportive partner who isn't on the same page, or if you disagree over how to pay off the debt and when, or what to save for and what to spend money on.

Jason and I communicated often about our goals, our dreams, and our stresses. We were willing to be candid about how we were feeling and what our needs were. We didn't second-guess each other's motives or actions, and didn't try to control the other's behavior. We knew we were on the same page.

If you and your spouse are *not* in a healthy place or able to manage your finances together, consider seeing a marriage counselor or financial professional who can help you through this process. Money is one of the top three causes of marriage problems and divorce and is not something to be taken lightly.

If you aren't married, please don't do this alone.

I understand that technically you have to do it alone with your income, but connect with someone you can trust and keep them updated on your highs and lows. Taking on something this important is worth sharing. Be straightforward about what you need (accountability, cheerleading, boundaries, or otherwise) and set up your support system and your team.

whittling down; way, way down

After we started doing the new budget and agreed on the plan for handling our income, we looked at ways to cut down our expenses. This was the second least fun part of the process, after the obvious part where we gave all our extra income to the loans.

First we were delusional, thinking we couldn't possibly cut down on or cut out any expenses. *We don't have car payments! No credit cards and no outstanding debt! Just the loans; what else needs cut? Isn't it enough that we're saying goodbye to so much extra cash each month?*

No, it wasn't enough. Because we could try harder, trim more, and achieve our goals faster.

Here is what whittling down our expenses looked like.

We already didn't (and still don't) have cable TV or a landline phone. We considered renegotiating our Internet package and speed and found we already had the cheapest plan. Our rent is set in stone and is raised only once every year.

We evaluated our entertainment subscriptions and kept the ones we used the most, and every so often we look at deals to get a free years' worth, or for options to pay yearly and lower the overall cost. These amounts are small in comparison to other expenses, but a dollar we didn't have to pay was a dollar we could give to the loans, and each one mattered.

We looked at our car insurance plans each time we got a new car (paid cash for, of course), and evaluated what we did and didn't need on the plan. We also pay our premiums every six months, saving us an amount through the full payment option.

If you aren't sure you're getting the best, lowest costing insurance, check out other companies and then call your current provider and ask what they can do for you. Leverage the fact that you're shopping around and you'd be surprised to hear what deal they can offer if you stay with them. This isn't rigging the system, this is business; this is your life. You are entitled to the best deal you can find and if they don't want you as a customer, I promise someone else will.

We changed our electric energy provider to cut down that cost. The company we used could change their rates whenever they wanted and we knew we could find a better deal with another company.

Again, maybe only a few dollars here and there, but remember when twenty dollars was once a big deal?

The biggest expense we trimmed was our phone bill. For years we carried the same phone plans most people do: we paid for the service and paid the monthly amount on our smartphones. It was about two hundred dollars for us both, and once a phone was paid in full that extra amount was taken off the bill.

But then I read about another phone service provider from a blog. I trusted this blogger's word, especially considering she lived on a boat year-round and had been using the provider for months. We researched the company and shopped the rates. That same month we paid the balance on our phones to buy them from our provider, canceled our plan, and switched to the new company.

We've had great service, and the best part is each plan is twenty dollars a month for the data we need and the other inclusions most plans have. We pay our plan yearly, meaning we went from $2,400 a year to $480 a year. And because the company utilizes SIM cards, if something happens to our phones and we get another one (like I did during this time, a refurbished iPhone for less than $250), we can put the card in the new phone and our plan transfers with it.

The hardest part of the budget to trim was our groceries. We enjoy food and we prefer variety. I'm not a fan of boxed pasta, one of the cheapest meals to make. I don't like eating the same thing everyday, which is usually another way to save money and cut down on the food bill. We like buying fruit often, even the pricier kinds. We choose some name brands over generic.

I'm sorry to say that this section won't cover how-to tips for meal planning, batch cooking, coupon clipping, buying in bulk, or other common budget busters.

We decided to be somewhat realistic during this process: If we had to cut everything else but needed one thing normal to keep us sane, the food would be it. What we did do is say goodbye to eating out. Not necessarily take-out, but eating out in a restaurant that requires sitting down and leaving a tip. (By the way: if you can't leave an appropriate tip, you shouldn't be eating out.)

Because we decided to be more lenient with our grocery spending, I tried to do it more mindfully.

What were we actually going to eat in a week or for the next three days? Which store was cheaper or what produce stand served a better product and helped a small business we valued? Which foods were in season, likely meaning they were less expensive (and better tasting)? How could I utilize what we had left over and clear out the shelves before buying new? When did a meal become more money than it was worth to buy and make, when all I had energy for was ordering a cheaper pizza? But on the flip side, how could we eat foods that were healthy for our bodies and sustained our energy?

It's funny, almost ironic. This is the one area we let ourselves keep open to spending, but it was also the area I ended up caring about evaluating the most.

We began to value our food more and found we didn't need ice cream in the freezer all the time. We didn't need to eat meat at most meals. We could do without dairy or use it sparingly. Potatoes are versatile; chili is cheap and delicious; rice is filling; getting a discount on a meal at work was cheaper than packing my lunch.

If you total all the ways we trimmed our expenses, it adds up over time. All that money was essentially being "thrown away" and now we could repurpose it and use it for the debt instead. We are still always looking for ways to do this easily and sustainably.

We did add one item to our budget, and I advise you do the same.

This item is life insurance.

If you don't have a form of life insurance and you have people in your life or household who depend on your income (spouse, kids, whoever), get it today. Do not wait until it's too late. Term life insurance is cheap.

We didn't have life insurance when we got married because until that "I do," no other person was depending on our income. But then our lives and our finances became combined and we were dependent on one another to share these burdens.

We learned about the need for life insurance in the same way we learned about the need for the smoke detectors we have: through stories of loss, sadness, and regret. The stories that are painful to hear, but infinitely more painful to live.

Life insurance is like some of the vaccines you get before you travel to, say, Africa: you may not get sick or come into contact with any form of disease, but better safe than sorry. In the same way, you hope you never need the money from a life insurance policy, but you don't want to find out you do after it's too late.

The part about life insurance that is most important to us is that for the most part it picks up the bill of a lost income if something happens to the policy owner. If something terrible happens to Jason or I (as in, one of us dies...), the other person will be debilitated by grief and put into a chaotic life with just one income.

As much as we did not want to add to our expenses, we understood the severity of this situation and agreed that we weren't messing around when it comes to events like these.

I'll be transparent: our term life insurance policy is twenty bucks a month per person and each policy is for five hundred thousand dollars. We followed the recommendation to take out policies ten times our annual incomes.

Not even a twenty-dollar problem can get in the way of that coverage.

To add it to the budget, I had to push aside any excuses. I could stop spending money out, buy a cheaper brand of shampoo, color my hair myself, not buy a new video game for Jason, and buy our cat less treats (we still feed her, obviously).

Whittle down your budget, but be mindful of what is most important, even if that means adding a new expense to the mix. Don't leave your family or spouse without an income and do not let them do the same to you.

sinking funds

Not a play on words. Not meant to be witty.

Sinking funds are for the piles of money you save for purchases outside of your regular budget. These can be purchases with a due date (like Christmas, which comes the same day every year, if you have forgotten); purchases you want to make when the fund is completed (a car, a laptop, a gaming system, new furniture, anything); or purchases that you make from time to time and want available money for whenever you want to make them (clothing, movies, books, a massage, anything of that sort).

Sinking funds are exciting because when you need the money it's already there. It's been saved and set aside and you get to spend it guilt-free. They're also exciting because saving money intentionally for a purchase feels motivating and purposeful.

I get no joy from making my rent payment, as much as I love our apartment. But I definitely love completing a savings goal and then getting to do something with the money I saved.

When we were getting out of debt, we wanted all of our extra income to go to that goal. But we knew we had large expenses in the future and we wanted to be prepared for them.

We had sinking funds for both of our new cars, my schooling programs, a vacation, tax bills, a new mattress, Christmas, and any other expense over five hundred dollars. We knew we could have paid for these things with our extra monthly income, but part of our budget was planning for these expenses and not letting them interfere with our debt repayment.

Severely limiting our debt payments for weeks or months at a time would have felt disappointing and slowed our adrenaline rush from making progress. Setting aside money incrementally instead helped us keep our enthusiasm and motivation and didn't derail our focus.

The best part about budgeting your sinking funds is that you can do it however you want to. You can save a certain amount monthly, per paycheck, weekly, or daily, or in any other method. You can save it as cash or move it into a different account, or any way that keeps the money separate from your recurring bills and emergency fund.

When we saved for Christmas, we decided how much we would budget to spend, divided that by ten, and saved that amount each month. Then, by the time October came and we wanted to start buying gifts, we had all the money we needed and it didn't affect our debt payments (and we didn't spend more than we needed or wanted to).

Let me tell you, a guilt-free Christmas is extremely enjoyable.

For some sinking fund goals we focused on a goal at a time based on what we had to buy first. For others without due dates we put in a certain amount each month and changed it if we needed to. Every time I got a paycheck I put ten dollars into a clothing sinking fund, or once a month I put five dollars into a fund for any book I wanted to buy.

The sinking funds that were for leisure were my buffer between feeling drained and restricted by the budget.

As soon as I said I couldn't or shouldn't spend money on books, all I wanted to do was buy a new book. Having a small sinking fund curbed this irrational need without hurting the budget or interrupting our debt payments.

Our sinking funds were my sanity.

I could save for Christmas, buy someone a birthday gift, spontaneously grab a latte, buy a new car, deal with a tax bill without stress, and still know that our debt was being taken care of.

"winter is coming": the snowball method

Now, *that* was a play on words. It was terrible, wasn't it? I haven't watched Game of Thrones, but this was too perfect not to use when thinking about "the debt snowball."

So, step one was the small emergency fund.

Step two was getting out of debt.

But "getting out of debt" or "paying off all debt" is too vague for me, and it might be for you, too. It's a daunting task and it took us over two years. Surely it was more complicated than those four words.

Yes and no.

It was simple because we decided it would be the only financial task we would take on during this time. We did not contribute to our retirement accounts, invest in other ways, or save money for the future (beyond large upcoming expenses). The debt was our mission and where we placed our focus.

But our debt did not all come from one source. This is where it could become complicated.

We had debt for a household purchase (those smoke detectors I mentioned, I'm actually not kidding), Jason's student loans, and my student loans. My student loans were from three different schools and owed to one company, but comprised seven separate groups. They were all due at the same time, but each group had its own interest rate. Jason's loans had their own monthly payment and due date.

This meant we had three debt payments each month, all with different interest rates and final due dates.

This isn't even as complicated as it could have been. Imagine if we'd had car payments, credit card debt, a mortgage, a line of credit, payments on electronic devices (e.g., laptops and phones), or any other type of debt on top of our student loans. Suddenly the simplicity of "getting out of debt" is lost to juggling payments and dates and fees.

So how did we learn to juggle? How did we do it all at once? Simple. We didn't.

Enter "the snowball method."

We learned this particular method from Dave Ramsey. The strategy is to pay minimum payments on all the individual debts and then list all debts from smallest dollar amount to largest dollar amount and pay them off in that order. The smallest amount is paid first with leftover money from the budget. When this debt is paid in full, the next debt on the list is taken care of. This is done until each individual debt is paid and you become debt-free.

The snowball idea is seen when, by paying them smallest to largest and one debt at a time, the traction is gained as the money from the paid-off debt is put onto the next debt, and the snowball keeps rolling as it picks up speed.

Need an example?

We had monthly payments of $65, $350, and $400. Our smallest loan amount was $1,500 (this loan had the monthly payment of $65). When this loan was paid in full, the $65 that had been going to the monthly minimum was now going to the next smallest debt amount (in this case, $3,000). That extra $65 became more "snow" on the "snowball."

I know I said I would be as honest and detailed as possible about our story and what we did, so here are our exact details. (I hate vague examples, so I myself would prefer to read a real-life story.) Feel free to skim or skip if you get the gist of this.

Our household item debt was $1,500 with a monthly payment of $65.

Jason's student loan debt was $30,000 with a monthly payment of $350.

My student loan debt (three schools, seven total loan groups, all paid to one company) was $68,000 with a monthly payment of $400 (the total debt paid with interest was $74,000).

My seven individual loan groups were the following amounts (smallest to largest): $3,000; $5,500; $7,000; $8,000; $10,000; $13,000; and $21,500. (I want to add that some of these amounts already had interest that accrued while I was in school. When all was said and done, I paid close to $10,000 in interest.)

Each month we paid minimum payments. The first debt we took on was the $1,500. All of our extra income went to paying this in full. When this was paid, its minimum payment of $65 (along with all extra income) went toward the next smallest debt, the $3,000. We repeated this process each time we paid off the next debt group. Because Jason's loan was one large sum, we paid that one last.

I think I know what you're wondering now.

Why didn't we pay each group in order based on which had the lowest or highest interest rate, as opposed to which had the lowest or highest dollar amount? If interest kept accruing, wouldn't it make sense to pay off those debts first and keep the interest from adding up even more?

This does make sense when you do the math. But we needed more than numbers and math to encourage us to keep going.

The list of individual loan groups was intimidating. We had around $100,000 of debt to get through. The interest was part of it, but our focus was on that big number. Beating the interest was a smart thought, but the feeling of accomplishing something was more motivating.

Starting with the loan with the highest interest rate would have meant starting with my $21,500 loan group. When we were brand new to this way of working, budgeting, and putting all extra income to the loans, this amount would have felt incredibly daunting. It would feel as if it took forever.

We knew what it felt like to experience financial success by achieving smaller goals (setting aside the emergency fund, for instance). That's the feeling we needed when that $100,000 was staring us down. I wanted to feel like we were doing something productive and checking a box off our insurmountable to-do list.

Our mindsets and our behaviors were more important than the numbers, the interest, and the math. Paying off that first $1,500 felt really good. We'd proven to ourselves that we could earn more money and control our money. We saw that we could sustain a small emergency fund (without using it) while *also* paying off $1,500 of debt. That was huge! We hadn't done that before!

Imagine what we could do if we kept going.

That's exactly what we did. We felt the success and the hope, we embraced our new reality of being able to pay off debt, and we were driven to take on the next amount.

Our second group of debt was my student loans.

The big picture was not pretty. That $68,000 was a nightmare to look at. The loan company had distributed each individual loan into a subgroup (groups A, B, C, D, E, F, and G), and each subgroup had its own interest rate. I used these groupings (with the amounts listed above) to determine which loan amount we would take on next (regardless of the interest rates).

Breaking the $68,000 down into smaller amounts was less overwhelming to look at. Mentally, I couldn't grasp the possibility of paying off $68,000, but I could handle, say, $3,000.

So that's what we did. We did what worked for us. We looked beyond the math and the logic and figured out what needed to happen in our mindset to make this possible.

We needed to feel we were making progress. Paying off the first $1,500 had done this. Paying off the $3,000 encouraged us even more. Each time we were close to finishing another group, we felt a rush of adrenaline and the healthy pride that fueled our motivation. The next loan group was always larger and more challenging, but we knew we could handle it, because look at what we accomplished so far!

The power of personal finances. *Personal.*

What you do with your money is your choosing. If you want to pay your debt based on the interest because this serves you and motivates you, then do that. If you want to tackle the largest loan first because getting it out of the way is what creates that adrenaline rush, then I applaud your determination.

Just do *something.* Make a decision. Stop staring at the numbers and wringing your hands, and put your money somewhere that helps you take another step forward.

Whether it's a snowball or an avalanche or the tip of the iceberg (again, the play on words; I'm sorry!), take action that leads to forward movement.

embrace the change

I don't like change. Not big change, at least. I can adapt to new or
pressing work situations, a shift in routine, or switching up a
laundry detergent if the kind I like isn't on sale.

But monumental life alterations and leaving comfortable
spaces makes sweat break out along my hairline. Just the thought
makes the room shrink a little bit, or ready to spin like a funhouse.

If you're not where you want to be or where you feel you are
meant to be, the success and life you're seeking will elude you. We
have to go after what we want and usually at a faster pace than
the one we're currently moving.

And sometimes this means we literally have to move.

It was time for *me* to move in jobs. The full-time job I had was
not where I wanted to be and was not taking me to that place
either. If I planned to commit wholly and seriously to this road to
debt freedom, I would have to make more money immediately.
The horse and buggy speed of income I was peddling would have
to shift into that of a Ferrari, or at least something with an engine
and wheels.

I had worked multiple jobs for the last six years, juggling
schedules and rarely taking a day off. But they didn't pay what I
needed them to. So I scaled my full-time job back to part-time
hours and accepted a new position elsewhere. An added benefit:
my previous full-time job was almost an hour's drive, whereas the
new one was five minutes. This would equal less gas to pay for and
fewer miles put onto the car.

More whittling down, one dollar, one expense at a time.

I was reluctant to start a new job. New co-workers, new customers, new responsibilities, new everything. I took a lot of experience in with me but I still had things to learn and room to grow.

This work toward debt freedom was shaping into more than just separating bank accounts and ordering fewer toppings on a supreme pizza. It was going to require every reserve of patience, energy, and balls-to-the-walls-ness we had.

Sometimes a definitive change like this can level up our commitment and efforts, even without our trying. It was a proverbial line in the sand for me: a clear divider between What Was and What Would Now Be. It was a chance to start over in more ways than one.

But that doesn't mean I wasn't nervous and intimidated by the changes.

I can go on and on about the poetry of fresh starts and taking leaps and "doing it scared," but altering life habits and doing something new is still that: doing something new. The comforting fact was that I could make changes again if these didn't work out. I could find a new plan, try another method, get another job.

We are always able to make changes and discover ways to transform our lives.

Keep your mind open to the reality of that poetry: fresh starts, small or big leaps, and doing it scared.

money comes, money goes:
facing the scarcity mindset

Money comes and money goes...straight to the debt.

Before I changed jobs and before we officially started my debt repayment, I picked my next education program. I would start in January and hopefully be done by the following December. We paid cash for this and it *had* to be The One.

We also decided *not* to keep deferring my loans while I was in this program. (*But deferring the loans defers the interest!* Yes, I know. We, myself included, become all about the interest and the smaller details when they're easier to look at instead of the intimidating big picture.)

I would love to tell you that at the time I had a great reason for not deferring them, but I didn't. I was lazy and didn't feel like finding and filling out the forms, sending them through the right channels, and waiting to see if the extended grace period would be approved. I also didn't know how to do this process until the last minute and said, *Whatever, I'll just deal with it.* (I do that a lot.)

But something good would come out of this, something I hadn't yet seen.

If I didn't defer my loans...if they came out of the grace period and had a due date attached...*I would have to pay them.* Soon.

I wouldn't be able to keep waiting, justifying, considering options or weighing imaginary pros and cons. I would have to do it whether I wanted to or not. I am grateful for this. This is the one time I've been thankful for my procrastination with paperwork (just this one time, I swear).

The first due date for a loan payment was set for April 2016, the same month I started my new job.

That first month became the first of thirty-two months where almost all of our extra income went to our debt. The money came in and it went right back out. It flowed through our bank accounts to the loan payments.

If I saw a dollar for more than a day it was because the processing time took longer over the weekend. If there was extra money in the account, it was being saved for something we had to cash flow or save for in a sinking fund (cars, taxes, online courses, Christmas, a vacation).

(Real quick. When I say 'cash flow,' in this context I mean that something had to be paid or saved for and we were paying for it from our income. We were 'cash flowing' whatever the thing was. Cash flow can also be a thing itself, like: 'My car engine dropped out while I was driving and I paid for the repair from our cash flow.' *(A true story? You know it.)*

This means that we didn't go into debt or pay for any of these things on a payment plan. That's also part of the 'cash' phrasing. We didn't literally pay for my car with physical dollar bills and cash; we paid for it without debt, financing, payment plans, interest, and without using our emergency savings fund.)

This way of money coming in and going back out became our new normal. Instead of being excited about the number in the bank going up, we learned to be motivated by numbers on the student loan website going down.

But at first it was terrifying to part with that much money. It shouldn't have been, because we weren't making this much money before, nor were we handling or saving it with care.

But now the money was coming in and what if something happened, what if our cars broke down before we could replace them, what if my laptop blew up, *what if all our socks had holes in the big toes and we couldn't wear them and had to replace twenty-seven pairs of socks and had to use the emergency fund because all our extra cash went to student loans?*

The scarcity mindset is a non-funny thing that can cause somewhat funny thoughts.

Having just enough (and nothing more) can suddenly feel like a reason to worry and become anxious. We hadn't experienced any emergency we couldn't cover, yet during the first few months of paying the loans I felt tense and nervous each time I made a payment.

Scarcity Me: "What if we need that money?"

Rational Me: "When did you need this much extra money before now? You didn't even have it before now!"

Scarcity Me: "Yeah, but...What if we just leave it in savings and keep it there in case..."

Rational Me: "In case what? The big toe sock thing? Pull yourself together."

Scarcity Me: "Ha. No. What if we keep it there until it reaches a certain amount and then pay the lump sum to the loans? Like a security blanket."

Rational Me: "You can do that if you want. But then you'll reach that number and it will be harder to part with the money than if you'd just done it each time it comes in. Are you planning on losing your job tomorrow? No. Is Jason? We certainly hope not! More money will come in. The emergency fund is always there. Trust your process. You had no qualms before when the process was broken. Embrace abundance and success instead of scarcity and fear."

Rational Me was right (she always is, it's annoying). Trust the process. Take the action you need to, even when the beginning of the process is intimidating and different.

Money will come and money will go, and it's up to you to decide which mindset to operate in.

if it rains, will it pour?

Another situation where we faced scarcity mindset was through dealing with unexpected costs that seemed to come up the month we officially committed all of our extra income to the debt payments.

Have you ever felt that the moment you commit fresh determination to make changes and pursue personal growth, struggles pop out of the woodwork and function like anchors trying to hold you down?

A friend recently told me about her decision to start setting new money goals. But within weeks of this resolve, she experienced those anchors weighing down her wallet. Her car needed fixed in more ways than one, her roof needed repaired in the near future, her credit card balance was more than expected, and other yearly bills were coming up. It felt like she couldn't gain traction despite her well-intentioned efforts.

I validated her feelings and frustrations and told her this was very common. I encouraged her to keep making efforts, and reminded her that over time the struggles would pass or at some point they would no longer feel like struggles.

The first three months of paying off our debt were not very exciting or motivating. We had just spent a large sum on my latest education program. Our tax bill had been higher than the previous year. We needed to set aside money to replace my car in the summer. We were debating saving extra money to replace Jason's car as well. We wanted to save for Christmas as early as we could.

Initially I felt deflated.

And then I felt the scarcity.

I couldn't slow down my thoughts and I wondered what would happen if these events didn't stop appearing.

What if we always needed to save for something else or had a new bill to pay or another car part to buy? What if we committed to this debt repayment and spent our extra money, but then needed it afterward for these sudden expenses?

I questioned the security of our emergency fund and the effectiveness of our budget. I felt constricted by our income. I wondered if we were smart to do this plan.

These thoughts came up a few times during those thirty-two months, but never so much as the first six. It took time to trust the process and to allow the results to prove this was working.

We had to move forward an inch at a time and believe that soon we would look back and find we'd traveled farther than ever before.

And once again, Rational Me was right.

Money will come and go. Cars will need replaced, expenses will be missed, and the budget might get messed up. The best money mindset is fueled by abundance, not scarcity.

And luckily, umbrellas are fairly cheap.

when forty isn't the magic number

Go to work. Get a J-O-B. Make money.

We're all taught this. We know it's an important part of adult life. We spend a lot of time figuring out how to do something that will make money and provide a livable wage.

But how much money? And how much work? Forty hours, right? Forty hours, five days a week, maybe Monday through Friday. ("Thank God it's Friday; Oh, God, it's Monday"...right?) Something like that.

But sometimes forty hours doesn't cut it. Sometimes the money made in forty hours isn't enough to cover expenses or to achieve financial goals. If this is the case for you (as it was for me), you have two options: make more money in forty hours or make money for more than forty hours.

I bet you know where I'm going with this.

It might be time to pick up some extra hours or a part-time job. Jason and I couldn't make more money in our forty hours, so we decided to make money for more than forty hours. He picked up overtime and looked for extra work on the weekend (yes, the sacred weekend). I picked up massive amounts of overtime and kept working the part-time job I already had.

We wouldn't be debt-free right now if we hadn't done this. Not even close. We might be sleeping more, watching more TV, having more social outings, spending more money, and coming home with our feet hurting a little less...but we wouldn't be debt-free.

Can I tell you a secret? *We don't regret missing out on any of that.* We can barely remember how that time felt, and it wasn't that long ago.

When we started picking up more work, we kept wondering when we would hit a wall. When would it become too much? Would we become angry (both with our situation and each other)? Would we go too hard and need to slow down and risk never going hard again? Would we miss out on parts of life we felt we couldn't get back?

Would becoming debt-free even be worth this intense effort?

I know it sounds too good to be true, but we didn't experience most of these negative side effects. Of course it was intense. Of course we wished we didn't have to do it. We slowed down occasionally and we had to negotiate this new lifestyle within ourselves and with each other. But it was worth it.

This way of living and working became our new normal. Our bodies and brains adapted to the changes. Working fifty-five to seventy hours was now an expected part of life. We told ourselves we could do this, that we *had* to do this, and that there was no other option.

Instead of feeling defeated by the number of hours required, we looked to the future and those future hours. One day this would be over. One day we would work less, sleep more, see each other more, and be completely debt-free. (Spoiler alert: for us that "One Day" is now every day.)

Committing to this debt-free goal also inspired extra work commitments, such as efforts towards raises and promotions.

It wasn't enough that we accepted overtime and took on side jobs. We wanted to commit to our work with the same energy and passion that was fueling our new attitudes and goals.

We both sought more responsibility in the workplace and gave attention and reflection to how we could become more involved and practice our all-in mindsets.

Mindset was everything. Mindset *is* everything.

Putting this enthusiasm into our work led to extra and larger raises, multiple promotions, positive reputations, and first-dibs opportunity for overtime.

"Yeah, but you're a crazy workaholic and you like *being at work that much, and I don't! I don't like being there the forty hours that I am now! I can't possibly add more hours or do something else on the side."*

I wish I had a better response to this. It's a variation of statements that have been said to me many times, and I've yet to craft a quality solution or answer that gives slack and supports lukewarm living.

I really want to say it's okay if you don't work more (even if you know you need to). I want to say it's okay to take your time with paying off debt or achieving other financial goals.

But if you want those goals to become reality sooner rather than later, something has to change. If you've whittled down your expenses and done what you can with your current income, but it just isn't enough, then that's the current reality you're facing. The forty hours isn't enough.

When it comes to personal finances and money goals, I am not a gentle, sensitive person. I'd rather rip off the Band-Aid than play with it until the edges are crusty and slightly lifted, but still too stuck to lift free from the skin. I like scalding hot showers and eat foods before they've cooled and chop vegetables too quickly, despite becoming faint at the sight of my own blood.

What I'm saying is, I hate lukewarm. I hate slow, partial efforts. I can't stand on the sideline of my own life and not go all in.

I wanted the results that would require more than forty hours. I wanted to achieve something that seemed impossible, something that would surprise even me.

I couldn't settle for forty hours when I could take on fifty. And when fifty wasn't enough, I took on sixty. Sixty felt good, but sixty-five felt better. Seventy was like flying and eighty propelled me to the stars. (Ninety was a bit much and ninety-five – for only two weeks, I swear – was a scary extraterrestrial euphoria I don't recommend.)

My hours varied from month to month, but what stayed the same was an underlying core value that sustained me: I always did all that I could for as long as I could. No more, no less.

Hear me out: You don't have to work seventy hours a week. You may not even have to work fifty hours a week.

But why doubt your capabilities before you've tried? Be your biggest fan and most valued supporter. Believe in your ability to try something new, something difficult.

If you can't get more hours at work, find them somewhere else. Pick up a side job doing something you enjoy if your current forty hours doesn't provide that. Start small if too much too soon seems unrealistic and intimidating. If you have to, do what I did and pick a new place to spend your first forty hours.

But at the very least, like with the debt snowball dilemma, try *something*. Those extra hours spent not working will be ready and waiting for you when you've achieved your goals and are ready to scale back.

How do I know this? Because mine were: I'm using them right now.

"no" is a full sentence

I spent the first half of my working years not saying No when I should have. I spent a lot of money and time on people, activities, and expenses that were unnecessary and could have been avoided.

Once I began taking on more working hours and had less extra time to give, there were fewer things to say No to. But "No" is still a full sentence and I had to learn to say it more than ever before.

The ability to say No is not wholly dependent on self-discipline or self-control. These are admirable qualities, but they won't sustain in the long term on their own. It's likely that something in you will rise up and want to rebel against these rigid gatekeepers. It will be easy (and feel good) to rationalize, justify, or bargain the act of doing the very thing you are trying not to do.

When the discipline and self-control run dry or are tested, having a clear purpose that reinforces your commitment is what will save your good intentions.

Purpose and commitment should be the driving forces behind a Why for saying No and delaying gratification or opportunity. We know why we need to say No. But we need to believe our reasons and stick to them at our weakest moments. Our belief sustains our purpose and commitment. We need to believe that the end result will be worth more to us than whatever we're refusing or putting off.

So when a sale pops up, when cold brew is half-price during happy hour, when appetizers are "buy one, get one," or when you've denied yourself for so long that you want to say Yes just for the sake of saying Yes, remind yourself of why you are saying No and why (for right now) it's more important and valuable to you than saying Yes.

We said No to family vacations (most vacations, period), to extra days off, to almost all social outings that were not family gatherings, to day trips with friends, to birthdays, to extra holidays, to spending big (or at all) on our own birthdays and wedding anniversaries. Anything that didn't align with our new goals had to be politely declined.

I don't regret any of it.

What I would have regretted was delaying our debt-free living by months or more just for the sake of saying Yes when we didn't need to.

Don't worry, I don't think saying No is easy. I don't expect you to think so either. And I am aware that at times it downright sucks.

In the current age we live in, with so much that we want put into our faces on a daily basis and everything at our fingertips, saying No to spending our money and time is harder than ever. Facing this leaves us feeling defeated and frustrated. Sometimes we're upset or angry that we can't say Yes to the life we want right now.

Saving money and attacking goals feels good, of course. But I won't lie and tell you that for the most part saying Yes to spending money and time tends to feel even better.

The problem and the reality is we need to earn that ability and privilege to say Yes. We need to work for the opportunity to do what we want with our money and time.

Once we do those things and we can say Yes, we understand why it feels good to say No. And then, hopefully, we can say No when we want to and not only because we have to.

In the future there will be time for vacations, days off, dinners out, social outings, concerts, better gifts, holiday celebrations, and more.

By saying No more often, Jason and I also began to value the times when we could say Yes.

Time with family felt more important than it had before. The one vacation we did take was appreciated rather than expected, and provided a greater satisfaction and time of rest. We grew closer to the friends we prioritized and enjoyed time out more than if it had been a regular and expected occurrence.

I also learned to say No to myself.

Before getting married I had spent most of my money on only myself. I could spend, save, do whatever I wanted, and it only affected me. But now there were two of us and that was more important than any purchase I'd made for myself in the past.

I learned what I did and didn't need. I set the boundary between what was a need and what was a want; between what had to be obtained Now and what wasn't required until Later or After.

I stopped getting my hair colored at an expensive salon. I didn't buy any new clothing unless I needed it (and I mean *needed* it, like, my work pants have holes them and it's not a good look; not needed, like, Oh no, I have "nothing" to wear and I know Target just flipped their clothing options). I stopped pretending to shop online for fun (this is especially depressing when you're giving thousands of dollars to debt each month), and I found cheaper brands for personal items.

I turned my attention to resources on money, personal finances, personal growth, and content that aligned with my current goals.

I also discarded the narrative that I *deserved* these things. That I had *earned* them.

What I deserved was a new financial future. What I was earning was our life of freedom and the ability to create our reality.

Saying No to myself became empowering because saying Yes to what mattered couldn't have been done without it. I don't miss what I said No to. Instead, I evaluate and say Yes to what is of lasting value to me, and I'm better for it every day.

one thing at a time

There is something to be said for doing one thing at a time. An argument to be made for narrowing focus.

But I'm bad at it. I really like multitasking. It feels self-important and high-powered. Like the more things I can "do" at a time, the more meaningful and productive my life is.

Being busy is a badge of honor I wore for years. I wore it for purpose and for meaning and for an excuse to say no to situations I feared.

Case in point: I have a TV show playing in the background as I type this. I pulled out my iPad to start a new show I've been thinking about, but as soon as it began I felt the need to do something with my hands, my eyes, my brain.

Then it occurred to me: *I can't just sit and watch a TV show. Why can't I do that?* I know part of me feels guilty for the "doing nothing" that watching TV seems to imply. But I also feel other guilt pressing against my ribcage: Be productive. Do something that "means" something.

There is science that proves multitasking doesn't help us, it distracts us. It divides and doesn't conquer. It does not always create success.

I tried to multitask with money, too.

I wanted to make money, spend money, save money, invest money, pay debt with money, give away money, and learn about handling money. All in the same breath and while doing fifty other things (of course).

(Now we are doing multiple things with our money, but none of that money is going to debt, and all of our income can be focused on goals that involve keeping the paychecks in our pockets.)

I've read about the hazards of multitasking personal finance goals. If we try to do it all at once, we can't make any one thing successfully stick. This seems to apply most accurately when debt is involved.

I scoffed and rolled my eyes when I learned the concept of focusing on one money goal at a time.

Oh, please. No multitasking? They haven't met me.

But now I think about what I feel like when I have a stack of tasks on a to-do list and a lot of ideas vying for my attention. I feel overwhelmed, under prepared, pressure to give equal importance and consideration to everything involved...and then I feel failure. Because it's likely I will fail.

Trying to multitask with money sounded like an intelligent, disciplined goal. The more we could do, the better we were, right? We spent most of our money, saved a little here and there, contributed to retirement, paid minimum balances on debt, and hoped the whole situation would work itself out.

But we didn't see that this multitasking was not accomplishing anything. We did not see that doing a lot did not equal a lot of progress.

When we decided to stop multitasking and to start achieving, putting our energy and income toward one thing at a time looked like this:

Stop contributing to retirement. In this case, we stopped the contribution only while we were getting out of debt. This is a sticking point for most people and I completely understand why. But pausing our retirement contribution for less than three years will not have kept us from our retirement goals. Instead, that income we contributed to retirement went back into our paychecks and into our budget (and, as you can guess, to the debt).

In hindsight, I acknowledge both the behavioral logic of this decision and our willingness to follow a proven plan fully.

But if I could go back and change something about this decision, I would have kept contributing as much as our companies matched and put the rest to our paychecks. Over time that money and the free money from our employers will multiply.

To challenge ourselves further to prove we valued this asset to our finances (a company match in a retirement plan), we could have cut down our expenses and spending even more to make up the small amount of retirement contribution we would have been missing from our paychecks.

Save a small emergency fund and *leave it at that amount* until becoming debt-free. I love the idea of having a large heap of money in the bank for my own mental security or for the ability to help a pressing situation, like a family member in need, without acquiring more debt or stress.

But multitasking our income while having debt made it hard to commit to noble goals like security blanket funds and charitable giving. We would save a little, find a "need" for it, spend it, and save again. Or we saved and then felt guilty that our debt was left sitting unpaid and accruing more interest.

We decided to commit to the small emergency fund and leave it at that. We needed to focus on our debt repayment, not on our savings plan.

Putting off this goal motivated us to get out of debt quickly so that we could get back to our other financial ambitions (like retirement, saving, and giving).

Pay each loan in full and one at a time. I don't want to say we had it easy, because there is nothing easy about repaying one hundred thousand dollars, but our debt repayment situation was simple (as seen in the debt snowball breakdown).

But we still had to decide in what order we would pay our loans. We could have chosen our order differently, either largest debt amount to smallest debt amount, or from highest interest rate to lowest rate. What mattered the most to us was that we did one loan at a time.

Commitment, focus, accomplish, repeat.

Hold off on charitable contributions or monthly donations. I have a separate section about this topic, but it was still a necessary part of our efforts to stop multitasking and start focusing.

We decided what percentage of our income we could continue to donate, and we committed to leaving it at that amount until we became debt-free.

I'm a firm believer that I cannot help someone if I haven't first helped myself, and it is no different with personal finances.

Learn *only* about what motivates the current goal. This one is not part of a financial plan. It's just something I did for my own mental sanity.

I love learning about any money-related topic and all things personal finance. I read about investment strategy, behavioral psychology, millionaire mindset, pros and cons of savings methods, and more.

But learning more about investment strategy during a time where I could not invest even the cost of a chai latte was... disheartening.

Thinking about the future moment where I could do this was encouraging, but it wasn't the inspiration I needed for my current goal. I needed to learn about the best methods for cutting down on electric usage, or how to stretch a grocery budget into the next week.

Instead of scrolling through blogs that detailed a multimillionaire success story, I was better served by following accounts where people were doing the same thing I was doing: becoming debt-free.

I would have plenty of time to learn about the new Vanguard retirement funds or which high-yield savings account would be best for our large savings goals. For now, I needed to focus my behavior, my energy, and my learning.

One thing, one dollar, at a time.

sharing is self-caring

The people who know me may not know this, but I used to hate telling people what I'm "doing" with my life. I don't jump at the chance to talk about myself and I don't seek to be the center of attention.

So I'm sure you can imagine the proverbial hurdle I had to get over when people became interested in what we were doing, or were concerned about why I was working so many hours. (I've worked a lot in the past, but when you say you just worked a hundred-day stretch, people get a little worried.)

I had to learn to talk about myself and share the current story of my life. It sounds petty, but it was difficult. Not everyone you talk to about your life is going to be supportive. Some people will question you, disagree with you, offer unsolicited advice, and knock you down where you're standing. They'll say you're not being realistic or you're not doing it the way they would do it.

But I guarantee there *are* people in your life who will support what you're doing and will do their best not to pass judgment or respond negatively.

During the first year I updated people verbally and only when asked. I didn't start a conversation with our goals or text out debt payment updates.

It was hard to admit how much we owed. Student loans are something of a joke ('We all have them; run me over with a car so they're paid for!'), but it was hard not to feel judged after saying I had over a certain amount. *Especially* when the paid work I was doing had nothing to do with the degree I obtained with those loans.

But at some point in the first year I realized that what we were doing was different and slightly unheard of. I didn't know anyone else working like we were or paying off debt as quickly. People had heard about becoming debt-free, but the responses to our progress were close to shock and awe.

I don't say this to brag. If anything, it surprised and encouraged us. This was normal to us now and I forgot that it wasn't normal to most other people.

If I was encouraged by our progress, was it possible someone else could be, too? If our success was seen more often, could it become normalized? Could somebody look at us and say, "I could do that."?

I wouldn't know until I took action to find out.

Year two I decided to start posting loan updates on Instagram and Facebook.

I had seen accounts dedicated solely to paying off debt and sharing stories and updates and it fascinated me. These people had found a community and a place to share their progress. It was inspiring and motivating, and it was there that I found my answer: yes, someone could look at us and say, "I can do that."

But first I had to show them what we were doing.

I posted updates for my part of the loans and for the combined total of our loans. I did a monthly update for the total amount and a post for mine whenever I felt the drop in numbers was significant. It was fun to find different backgrounds and fonts and decide what parts of the process to talk about. It was even better to receive the positive feedback and support from the people who "liked" and commented on our updates. I loved when people asked me questions or messaged me for details.

The more I shared about our story and our progress, the more ambitious I became about our goals. I wanted to show the numbers going down quicker and wanted to prove that what we were doing was a good thing. I answered questions and pointed people to resources and became a cheerleader for the same people cheering for us.

As much as I was doing this for me, I'd like to think I was partly doing it for them, too. I didn't want to tell anybody what to do; instead, I wanted to show them what could be done.

But it wasn't all sunshine and rainbows, and I was careful not to paint this picture.

I wanted people to see an update and feel inspired, but I didn't want them to think it was out of reach or that we were perfect or better than them. Sometimes I posted an update with content that told more than the basics of how we were doing. I shared our struggles, our sacrifices, the low moments, and the hurdles we came up against. I showed that what we did really is possible for anybody else.

Share your goals and your progress. Tell the people closest to you what's going on and the changes you're making to create a new and debt-free life. Seek out support and encouragement and don't be afraid to publicly share it on the Internet in a safe place. There is strength in numbers.

I once thought we were doing this alone, but I was wrong.

My only word of caution is to be wary of over-sharing with people you know who will be negative or unsupportive.

You should feel pride in how you're living and not be afraid to share it, but that doesn't mean you have to invite the naysayers or a damaging presence into your story. If people become toxic toward you, feel free to side step them and ignore the things they say.

If they question your methods or your choices, be patient instead of defensive in your response. Oftentimes we raise issues over things we don't understand, or we reject a lifestyle we aren't willing to choose for ourselves. We can become intimidated when we see someone else leveling up or doing more than we're able to. It's easy to attack and be negative, or downplay success and assume it's all luck and chance.

If and when people behave this way, remember where you were before you started, and try to offer grace.

minimalism

A lot us (myself included, once upon a time) roll our eyes when we hear the word minimalism. We think, "Oh great, I have to get rid of all my stuff and not buy new things, and I'm not allowed to enjoy owning material possessions, and I'm terrible for giving and getting Christmas gifts."

Hold on for a second.

I learned about minimalism while we paid off the loans. I didn't look into it as a way to make more money, spend less money, or anything related to our debt-free efforts. But once I put it into practice, I decided they were related, at least to me.

For me, minimalism is more than a daily practice or a challenge to get rid of personal items. It's a mindset (and you know I love a good mindset). It is the ability to experience life and joy apart from what I own and what money can buy me. It's the power to say no to shiny object syndrome. Being free of the Fear of Missing Out (we'll get to that, too).

To practice our minimalism, we looked at our apartment, our furniture, and our possessions.

What did we own that was unnecessary or taking excess space? What did we have duplicates of? What did we hold onto for the sake of nostalgia, and did we need to keep these items? Did we have extra furniture that we kept for "someday" that we didn't need?

I always thought I was good at keeping my clothing and personal possessions at a minimum. I wasn't a pack rat, I didn't hoard, and I knew when it was time to let go of the past. But we had a LOT of stuff we didn't need.

Over the course of a few weeks we went through the entire apartment room by room, talking about what we needed and what was extra, what was taking up too much space and what we could replace later on if we needed or wanted it again.

We sold furniture, threw out junk, gave away duplicates, parted with nostalgic items we attached way too much meaning to, and set boundaries on collecting and acquiring new possessions.

Looking for specific examples? (As always, feel free to skim or skip if you aren't.)

We downsized furniture and appliances: sold a bedroom furniture set we didn't need, got rid of couches and chairs we didn't use, sold book shelves and a desk, and parted with appliances we kept for "what if" scenarios.

We gave away and donated duplicate kitchen utensils and excessive plates, bowls, cups, glassware, silverware, and coffee mugs. (I only kept my favorite...fifty? *Yikes.*) I tossed old notes and textbooks I no longer used and donated over two hundred books (maybe more, I wish I had counted).

Getting rid of my books was my biggest challenge.

I love owning books, I love seeing them on my shelves; but I didn't need and would never read most of them again. I kept them out of habit and because of misplaced attachment. I liked the idea of them more than their actual value and contribution to my life. I didn't need books I read in middle school or a series of forty books I found at the library during a year-end sale.

I kept twelve books from the shelf and two years later I still haven't regretted getting rid of the others. (Perspective: I donated them to my local library, so if I want to read them again I can check them out.)

We threw out excessive office supplies and old paperwork; organized each space and evaluated every item we owned; went through bathroom supplies and personal toiletries; threw away half-used candles and outdated décor; gave away old toys and stuffed animals; and tossed extra blankets, sleeping bags, and sets of bedding we would never use.

We went through our clothing and identified what we wore regularly and what we kept for "just in case." I got rid of bags and bags of clothing I didn't remember buying, and unearthed some pieces I forgot I had. Jason tossed shirts and pants from high school and discovered he actually needed more new clothing to make his wardrobe better equipped for the coming seasons.

We also set boundaries for what we would acquire in the future or what items we were willing to keep for the sake of nostalgia and collecting.

The collection I kept was my specialty coffee mugs. They are not valuable. They are not rare or special. But I like how they look and we have been able to keep them without taking up space we need for something else. I could get rid of them today if I had to.

That's my core essence of minimalism and how I practice it.

I do not need these items and I do not feel unhealthy attachment toward them. I can see them for what they are: pretty trinkets, fun to collect and use, an added décor to our living spaces, and in no way necessary to my life and wellbeing.

Getting rid of this much stuff (and for the right reasons) felt *so good.* We had more space, better organization, and experienced freedom from our attachment to material belongings. I am more than my coffee mug collection. We are more than our apartment décor and fancy kitchen appliances.

If we had to, we could pack up tomorrow with a few necessary belongings, our cat, and start somewhere new. A fire or other disaster that took away our possessions would be upsetting, but not debilitating.

We repeated this process every few months until we knew we couldn't get rid of anything else without tossing things we genuinely needed and wanted.

But even now I go through each room from time to time, finding the odd item or piece of clothing that isn't serving a purpose and is no longer needed in our home. It still feels good. I can look around the apartment and know that our creature comforts aren't suffocating us.

How does this relate to becoming debt-free?

When we decided to minimize and set boundaries, we also confronted personal desires to buy new or excessive things. If we weren't as tempted to buy, that equaled less money we would spend.

This was the most important benefit of minimalism for me. I like the things I own, but I can always find something new and "better" to fill a material void and create a minute of happiness. Spending money leisurely or for enjoyment can trigger my brain like a sugar high, and that temptation made me nervous.

Confronting this has made a world of difference, especially in our efforts to change our personal finances.

Practicing these minimalistic behaviors and spending habits has also inspired contentment, a true satisfaction neither of us had experienced until this process. We liked who we were and what we had, but we always knew we wanted more or better. But what we had was perfectly adequate, and if it hadn't been for seeing something else, we wouldn't have felt a need for more (or "better").

I'm not saying any other person has to do this to create financial success. But this is our story and I said I would tell you everything we did that contributed to our debt freedom.

Without this part of our story, we would still own hundreds of dusty books, five identical wooden spoons (I still need to know how I acquired so many), clothing from seven years ago, a second bedroom full of furniture and functioning as storage space, and so much more.

FOMO

Fear Of Missing Out can be an ugly, unsettling feeling.

It starts out innocently enough: you weren't invited to something and you wish you had been; you saw a social media post that made you feel left out or as if your life is lacking something; you hear about another person's significantly higher pay and you daydream the ways you would spend that money if you had it (and maybe you begrudge them a little, too).

The initial innocence can give way to regret, to inability to take action, to second-guessing, to making rash decisions that only bring more regret. Sometimes it can lead to anxiety, to risky behavior, or to feeling pressure and burden because of shame and comparison.

There's a lot of "What If?" in the middle of FOMO.

What if I had that; what if I was like this; what if (fill in the blank) would happen to me? Lurking behind the "what if" is the insecurity, the scarcity, the comparison, and the self-deprecating mindset.

Behind all of that is the fear or idea that if someone else has "more," then you have "less." This could be more or less of anything: money, opportunity, passion, happiness, love, beauty, positive memories, fulfilling work, chances to start over, or anything else we think to compare to another person.

Making significant changes to our lifestyle stirred up a lot of FOMO inside me.

At times I was afraid we would miss out on important or fun parts of life because we were working so many hours. I was afraid to miss out on special sales or supposed "one time only" opportunities because all of our income was already spoken for. I feared losing the chance to travel while we were young because our financial plan would put travel into the distant future.

Fear of missing out could have slowed me down, if I let it. I could have acted on it, or not acted because of it, and ruined our efforts to become debt-free in the timeline that we did.

It tried to work its ugly sorcery through more than my mindset and financial plan. It also appeared to me in social media, in financial ways, and through relationships and friendships.

Social media. Sharing our updates and story on social media was nerve-wracking and exciting, but it also made me question my motives and my own FOMO issues.

Was I doing this to show off to someone else? Was it okay to post if it made someone feel insecure or the urge to compare our lives and situations? Did it matter either way, since I can't control how another person feels or interprets my message?

I decided to be transparent. I wouldn't sugarcoat our story or make us look self-important. I wouldn't let anyone come away with the idea that we were lucky, extra #blessed, or doing something no person had done before.

For the sake of my own FOMO, I only followed social media accounts that challenged and inspired me. If I saw a post and felt shameful of our story and our debt, I would "unfollow" and refocus. If I negatively compared our efforts instead of being open to learning and observing, I would reconsider my need to look at other people's lives.

Financial. Much of my financial FOMO is more than fear. It's rooted in my jealousy and insecurity and the feeling that what I'm doing is not "enough."

It was hard to watch my peers earn more income for half the number of hours I was working. I was happy we were doing smart things with our extra income, but I still felt a loss for opportunities I saw but didn't have. I feared that I was inferior and not worthy of a higher income without an intense work schedule.

My financial fear of missing out also came to me in feelings of uncertainty: were we right to put off retirement, emergency savings, investing, and charitable giving?

It spoke to me in a "What if" narrative and I hated it. What if we missed out on compound interest? What if we didn't invest when the market was "hot"? What if someone needed our help and our income was tied up in debt? What if something unexpected and terrible happened and we needed much more than our one thousand dollar emergency fund?

These irrational fears paralyzed me.

I had to seek clarity and stick to our plan. I hadn't given a moment of concern to these issues before we started this process...why did they consume me now?

Scarcity and FOMO. Working together and working against me, both created in my mind and now waging war in my mind.

Personal relationships. The majority of my FOMO here can be explained in the childhood experience we've all shared: we don't want something until we see someone else have it; and if they have it, we can't have it, and then maybe they shouldn't get to have it either.

I've felt this FOMO plenty of times before trying to become debt-free. The difference this time was now I had money, a lot of money, and I could get the things I saw and wanted. Some online shopping, an exciting vacation, a table at a new restaurant…I could keep up with my friends and their lives if I wanted to. I could go out with them and buy what they owned and get rid of FOMO once and for all.

But I didn't. And I can't.

Fear of missing out will always be there, even if I know the ways to live around it and act without it. There will always be something more, newer, and better to want. People in my life will always be living their own lives, and at times I'll struggle against the desire to emulate.

Wanting something because I saw someone else have it is not a good enough reason to want it for myself. It's okay to be ambitious, to level up, and to set goals that look like someone else's. But I needed to (and still need to) work toward something because *I* wanted to, not because I saw someone else with it.

The good news about FOMO is it's all in our heads. We experience physical symptoms and the fear can make us think or do crazy things, but it's still up to us to decide whether or not to act on it.

Fear of missing out will always be nearby.

We can call it jealousy, envy, or insecurity and comparison, but it all boils down to the same: we fear we are missing out on something another person has, or fear we are missing out on an opportunity we'll never get back.

The other good news is we all have choices. We can choose what we see on social media, who we follow and interact with in real life, and how we handle our personal finances.

We can choose to believe that we aren't missing out after all.

when giving it all...is there a way to give even more? (charitable giving on a debt-free journey)

Do you want to know the best part about making a budget? I may have mentioned it before, but it's worth repeating.

The best part about making a budget is that *you control where the money goes.*

The money does not control you. The expenses do not haul you away in handcuffs, set a bail, and await the payment. The money is not held at ransom in your checking account, demanding anything in return besides the work you did to earn it.

As individuals and as a couple, Jason and I value charitable giving and altruistic opportunities. We like to sponsor missionaries we know, donate to nonprofit charities with missions that inspire us, and give money to churches and companies serving our local community.

But with our income tied up in our debt-free intentions, could we fund this part of the budget without feeling irresponsible (or worse, regret)?

The way we answered this question should not be how every person would answer.

Each household budget looks different. If our income just barely covered our expenses, we would say no, we could not responsibly fund the charities. Our debt had to be our core concentration and putting it off did not serve this focus. But because our income exceeded our expenses by a certain amount, we chose to give in small ways until becoming debt-free.

Does it sound selfish when I say we needed to focus on our own financial goals before considering giving to charity or to those more "in need" than ourselves?

At first, I thought it did. I felt ashamed of my debt and my spending choices that made me unable to help noble causes and support people around me.

But then I reminded myself the importance of becoming debt-free as quickly as possible.

The more income we freed up, the more we could save, spend, and *give*. Allowing the interest to accrue on my debt just to do more charitable giving was not a financially intelligent choice. Before I could help others, I needed to help myself.

You know the saying: you can't pour from an empty cup. And being in debt emptied my cup. Trying to throw our income at everything kept it from refilling. Over-contributing during this time would be more like charitable spending than charitable giving.

Thankfully, there are ways to give besides giving our money.

We can give our time, our energy, our extra resources, our awareness, and our compassion.

things we didn't do

I get it: you're reading this to see what we DID do, not what we DID NOT do.

But there are a lot of helpful things to do to become debt-free that we chose to leave out of our own process. We didn't forgo them because they aren't good ideas; we just didn't feel the need to do every single thing there is to do.

We wanted to keep our methods simple and uncluttered. Sometimes information overload keeps us from moving forward or becomes a distraction from taking action. Sometimes it's best to go deep instead of wide.

Cash envelope system. We learned about this from Dave Ramsey and I've seen it followed all over the Internet. I even bought a special wallet to try it. I'm glad I tried it because I found out it wasn't for me. I didn't have to spend any more time wondering if I was missing out on a great method (yes, I even feared debt-free FOMO).

The envelope system is simple and focuses on utilizing cash as the primary method of payment.

The basic premise: Take out the majority of the budget's expenditures in the form of cash, divide the amounts into different envelopes (literal envelopes or otherwise), and commit to spending no more for that category when the cash from that envelope is gone.

For example: If you budget $100 for going out every two weeks, put the cash into the envelope at the beginning of the first week, use *only* that cash for going out, and when the cash runs out there's no going out until the next refill.

Using the cash envelopes is a powerful way to adopt discipline with the budget and spending. It tests the ability to commit to a plan and say No when the cash is gone. Swiping a plastic card and entering bank information online is very easy. Sometimes parting with cash (especially limited cash) is not.

The best way to test this theory is to go grocery shopping and only take cash. You're likely to evaluate each item and price point in a way you haven't before.

If you choose to incorporate this method, there are a lot of ways to have fun with it and make it interesting.

Instagram and Pinterest have an infinite amount of accounts and posts dedicated to cash envelopes and budgeting with this method. You can find printable cash envelopes (vertical or horizontal) in a never-ending variety of patterns and designs; budget binders and cash envelope trackers; Filofax wallets and other types of cash envelope wallets; and tutorials on YouTube and Facebook.

Budgeting and becoming debt-free does not have to be a drag and there is a growing community dedicated to proving that.

Consolidate loans. Loan consolidation sounds great: one "easy" payment, one interest rate, and one company to worry about paying.

We learned not to consolidate loans unless the new overall, total loan will have a lower interest rate than before consolidation. If I had consolidated my loans, the rate would have been more than my highest rate (doubled!) on some of my loans.

Times where this may be the best option for student loans are when they are from different providers, especially if some (or all) are private and some are federal. Private loans tend to have higher interest rates than federal and not all loans offer the same method of repayment.

If you're thinking about consolidation, look closely at these details before you do it.

And don't be too quick to pat yourself on the back when you consolidate: you still have work to do and debt to get rid of.

Rice and beans. I touched on this topic earlier when I talked about ways we cut down on expenses, and that cutting down on food cost wasn't always one of them.

"Rice and beans" is what we think about when we consider how to eat as cheaply as possible. We applaud those who reduce their grocery bill to nothing in order to put more money to the debt.

That being said, until recently we've rarely eaten "rice and beans." We didn't live off peanut butter and jelly. I don't like canned tuna. I've never had a pack of hot dogs in our freezer. We don't buy boxed macaroni and cheese.

I know: we sound like food snobs. We're not!

We buy discount groceries and look for sales and choose generic when it doesn't make a difference in quality. But we didn't force ourselves to buy foods we don't like in order to save money.

If you like any of the foods I just mentioned, buy them and eat them! But if you don't like them, accept my permission to forgo them. Food can be one of the finest pleasures life has to offer us; we're not afraid to spend more on it when we want to.

"But what about coupons?"

Nope. We don't clip them. Not ever. Not a single coupon. We have old ones on our fridge we've forgotten about (I just checked; still there). I don't have the patience for it. If clipping coupons has value to you, if it's your Thing, do the thing.

Enjoy your process to the best of your ability, just like we enjoyed ours.

some unsavory moments (the ugly parts)

This section isn't meant to scare you away from changing your financial story and becoming debt-free. But I did say I would tell you everything.

We had a lot of cheerleaders come alongside us. Our families were proud, our friends were encouraging, and the social media community was inspiring.

But not every word that reached my ears was kind.

If you read this and take one piece of advice, take this one: think before you speak. Sometimes you need to keep your opinions to yourself. I'm not an everybody-gets-a-trophy-for-being-alive person, but uninvited negativity can hurt.

Working as much as I did raised a few eyebrows and attracted unnecessary commentary. I understood the curiosity and the concern, but I did not approve of or excuse the following comments:

"When does your husband see you? Is he okay with you working this much?

"Do you ever make dinner? What does he eat?"

"How can you be a good wife while you work this much?"

"Is the house a wreck? Who is washing dishes and doing laundry?"

"You're going to burn out so badly. Hope it's worth it."

"That's what you get for so much debt and degrees you don't use."

"It's a shame you can't get a real job and make decent money."

"I hope you're not making him pay for your mistakes."

"Your poor husband."

I am not making any of this up. I had these exact words spoken to me, some of them more than once. People can be brutal and rude, and their words can be ugly.

On my hardest days, when I felt like this process would never be over, I took too much of this personally and I let it define me.

I felt ashamed, embarrassed, and scared: Were they right? Was I a terrible person and wife? Was Jason going to see this truth and leave me? Was being married to me worth this crazy debt and what it took to get rid of it? Was it wrong for us to combine incomes and pay our debt together? (I'm shaking as I type all of this because it puts me back into those awful moments of fear and shame.)

But instead of dwelling on the horrible feelings, let's clear some things up.

Jason and I saw each other plenty during this time. We live in the same apartment and I rarely worked more than a thirteen-hour day. Because my workday started at five a.m. or earlier, I was home before seven. Yeah, we were exhausted, but we still spent time together. We agreed on this plan and this schedule.

Did I ever make dinner...yes, most of the time. Can I tell you something, though? *Men can cook, too.* And if they can't, maybe they should learn. Maybe *everybody* should learn. Or maybe nobody has to cook and meals can be bought, ordered, delivered, or put together simply and without hassle. Jason eats whatever he wants to eat, just like the rest of us. His eating was not dependent on me providing it. And vice versa.

I won't address the good wife question. That was just rude.

As for the house being a wreck, it wasn't. Not ever.

Since we both live there and we're productive adults, we both take care of our living spaces and share these responsibilities. We both wash dishes, vacuum, do laundry, take out trash, and feed the cat. It's demeaning to imply a person is not capable of taking care of his or her own home.

I didn't burn out badly. Obviously, it was all worth it.

Don't *ever* tell someone they do not have a "real" job. You can think whatever you want, but keep thoughts like that in your head. The fast food places, restaurants, grocery stores, and gas stations we depend on aren't manned by robots (not yet, right?). Real people are working these real jobs. And unless robots take over this burden, we'd better hope this doesn't change, or many of us are (pardon my non-French) screwed.

The best part about the "real job" comments (which I received often) was that they came from people *as they were reaping the benefit of these services.* (If we all get "real jobs," who is going to make the coffee I served for three years?)

My poor husband. Yes, my poor adult self-sufficient husband who can feed himself and sustain his life without my assistance. My poor husband, someone you also just offended.

You know what's crazy?

Not one of these comments was said to Jason.

No one questioned him working sixty hours or picking up work on the side. No one asked him how the house was cleaned and if I was being fed. No one told him it was a shame he didn't have a degree for the debt he was repaying.

Hearing these comments were some of the worst moments while we paid off our debt. Working so much was painful and exhausting, but at least that served a purpose. Enduring unsolicited commentary did not.

I hope no one says these things to you.

If they do, I hope you can handle it better than I did. Keep your head high and keep going. Don't second-guess your actions or give the ugly commentary an audience.

debt freedom is not a fix-all

It's true that becoming debt-free and taking ownership and control of personal finances will influence other areas of your life.

It can be a catalyst to other changes and successes, but it will not fix everything. It will not cure most health issues, automatically solve relationship problems, make raising kids 100% easier, remove job stressors, or cause spontaneous, effortless weight-loss.

Will it help with all areas of life in some way? I believe so. But it will not fix everything all on its own.

I've heard the saying that when you make more money, if you don't first confront your issues to make changes, you risk becoming only more of what you already are.

So if you're unhealthy, you become unhealthier. If you have anger management problems, your anger becomes worse. If you spend all extra money on hobbies or entertainment, you'll only spend more than you already do.

This logic is part of why making more money does not assume you will do a one-eighty and be smarter with it, or that you'll pay off your debts (or not keep going into debt).

Becoming debt-free solved our *current* debt problem.

It did not protect us from getting back into debt or from other money problems. It did not shelter us from our own spending decisions and patterns that could require another intense process and sacrifice.

In the same way, becoming debt-free did not solve any other difficulties or frustrations. I still wanted to leave my job and do other work. I still had personal issues that took up mental space and added to the clutter.

I did believe, for a time, that achieving our debt-free goals would force everything else into a better place. I thought it would be a game of dominoes: one good thing triggering the next, and then the next, until our problems were solved and the future was bright and clear.

As per usual, I was wrong.

I still have personal issues to work on, just as we all do. I still fight against FOMO, consumerism, insecurity, and comparison. I still face daily financial decisions that could make or break our debt-free status and current money goals.

Becoming debt-free did not cure me of potential hardships.

Instead, it taught me that I can overcome them and that I can learn and make changes and grow.

perspectives on spending

Okay. Let's address this elephant in the room. If you don't see it yet, I promise at some point you will.

Spending money: When is it "okay," and do I need to justify it (to myself and to other people)?

Your money is yours.

You earned it, so theoretically you can do whatever you want with it: spend it all, save it all, invest none, lose some. You don't have to explain or justify any action to any person.

BUT. Life requires money.

Living requires spending, but we tend to call it "expenses" instead, as this is a more acceptable way of saying it. We don't say "I spent all my money already," we say, "I had bills to pay." We can understand paying bills. We all have them.

So, let's say your paycheck is gone because of rent, gas, insurance, phones, food, and keeping the lights on. No big deal. That's okay and accepted (maybe expected)...right?

But add in an iced coffee or some organic produce or dinners out and a craft beer and two concerts a month and another coffee mug to match the other thirty-two you've collected. Well, suddenly *those* purchases are frivolous and "unnecessary," and the spending wasn't "good" and we all have an opinion on it.

There's your elephant: perspectives on spending, certain spending being more acceptable than others, and the way our money leaves our hands being deemed "good" or "bad."

(Notice that I didn't say the *amount* of money being deemed good or bad. I said the *way* our money leaves our hands, meaning the things we spend it on.)

We can't actually save all of our money. We do have to spend part of it in order to live. That's the deal with being a human. Want a roof over your head? Need to barter for that privilege. Screens in each room and hand? Have to trade something of value in return.

Our barter and trade is done with money, with our income. That's the currency of the majority of our world today. There is almost no getting around it, so we might as well accept it and get used to it.

But we aren't expected or required to trade all of our money, and we get to decide where and how we trade it. I don't need an Instant Pot like I need electricity. I don't need all seven Harry Potter books and movies (*okay, yes I do*) like I need gas for my car. I don't need collectible mugs from Starbucks from every state I've visited...but I do need life insurance and health insurance.

I still have choices and the ability to determine what is a need and what is a want. My income is still my own to delegate. Yours is, too.

Going through the budget and whittling down expenses taught us that we actually *could* choose which expenses we pay for. We don't *need* Internet in our home, but we want it. We don't need our specific apartment, but we like it. We select every single item and service we pay for. Our money isn't ever leaving our hands and accounts without our say-so.

And neither is yours.

But what about the costs and the money spent beyond the budget? How do we handle those things? How do we make these purchases without feeling the need to explain or defend them?

Before we started paying off debt, I didn't bat an eye about spending money on things we didn't need. We made our money and we would spend it how we wished. Nobody watched or questioned our spending (that we knew of).

But as soon as we made it public that we were cutting down on spending and increasing income and paying it all to our student loans, somebody somewhere had an opinion about what we spent our money on. Sometimes we heard it, but most times we didn't.

How do I know this? Because I've been just like those people. We all have.

If a friend says she want to save money and then buys a latte, a lot of us watch this event and inwardly think, "*Oh*, I thought she was *saving* money." We become judgmental and superior and require that person to justify the expense. But if she were paying her water bill we'd never have those thoughts.

So once we publicly stated our goals, if we spent money on dinner out or bought a new juicer, I guarantee someone somewhere was having those judgmental, superior thoughts. "*Oh*, I thought they were paying off their debt. *That* spending seemed unnecessary."

I'm not saying this to shame you or myself. I'm saying it to be honest, and to send a reminder that we're all made of the same stuff. We're all trying our best, but sometimes we're acting and thinking at our worst.

All that to say, don't be concerned about what someone thinks of your spending or your money goals and habits. And equally, refrain from caring and getting worked up about theirs.

Unless you are a person's spouse or accountability partner, their money choices are not obligated to suit your opinions. Someone could be making the worst financial decisions and it's still none of our business.

A lot of people wanted to tell me how to get out of debt or how to spend or not spend our money. I *hated* it. I dreaded those conversations. I understand having your thoughts and opinions – I have plenty of them myself – but just keep them in your head and focus on your own life.

You don't need to explain or defend your spending. You only need to be aware of it, own it, and take responsibility for how it affects your finances and your life.

Another perspective about spending is to know what our money means to us.

Specifically, what value do we assign each dollar and how do we decide what is more valuable or appropriate? Do we compare these apples to apples? Is each dollar or expense equal? For my own money, I would say no, each expense is not "equal." Not every dollar is valued equally.

I know this because I value the money needed for rent more than the dollars I "throw away" on take out and another coffee mug. (I must collect them all!)

They're all earned in the same way and they all have the same monetary value, but I tend to treasure some and disregard others.

Why is this?

I actually have no idea. I'm sure there's psychology behind it, scientific evidence that says why we care more about our money for bills than we do for other spending (or vice versa, depending on your priorities), but I've yet to read up on it.

What I *do* know is that while we paid off debt I learned to adopt a new perspective on how I managed and spent our money.

Enter The Kitchen Gadget and The Work Shoe.

We have a lot of gadgets: they're all matching black and chrome, they're handy, and they all feel necessary. I look forward to buying them and I like the process of finding a home for them in the apartment (we're running out of room, by the way).

They seem like pricey items. "Big" purchases. Luxuries. I research each one extensively and compare models and reviews. Then we pick one and take the plunge and trade our money for this new gadget. It feels like such a process and as if we parted with *so much* money (and hopefully it was worth it!).

But yet when we eat dinner out we spend probably half the amount or more (tip included, always) on ONE MEAL and we don't blink an eye. And for special events and dinners we spend this same amount (or more).

What is the deal with this?

I just agonized over spending eighty dollars on a thing I'll use over and over again, but I'm throwing that down on *one* dinner and my palms aren't sweating? (Okay, they're kind of sweating right now; that better have been a great dinner.)

Then there were the expensive pairs of work shoes.

My entire working career has required black non-slip shoes (you know the ones). The typical options weren't durable enough anymore for a schedule like mine. They fell apart too quickly and didn't have the support needed for a fifteen-hour day.

I went through five pairs of these shoes in year one of becoming debt-free. It was a frustrating money suck. But I needed these shoes. I needed these shoes for this work for these hours for that money for the debt-free goal!

Why was I so opposed to spending the money on them – but I could justify *another* coffee mug or a book (or three) or an expensive brand of shampoo?

It was my perspective on spending.

I told myself that one type of spending was worse than another, or that one paycheck was more valuable than the next.

When these five pairs of shoes failed me, I finally admitted that I needed heavy-duty shoes despite the price tag. I hated paying that much for a pair of work shoes and I dreaded having to buy a second pair the next year. I felt guilty for spending the money "that could have gone to the debt."

But I had to confront and change my perspectives about spending. These shoes brought so much value to me, much more than two dinners out or another material consumption that would sustain me only temporarily.

I can't tell you what should be valuable to you, or what type of spending will or won't bring you joy and fulfillment. I can't judge your money or how you use it.

I have a friend who loves having her nails done. She loves how it feels; it's part of her self-care. She felt guilty for getting them done. ("I could have saved that money for X.")

But I tried to show her the perspective that although she agonized over getting her nails done, she didn't quibble about lunch out with me. Why not? They were the same price and each brought her value.

I also reminded her that in the long run that nail expense only added up to a certain amount a year, likely much less than she had been thinking in her guilt. It was also a quarter of *one* day of paid work, maybe less than that.

Her mindset for how to save and spend money was great. But what about her perspective on how to view her spending? Paying attention to that was equally important.

I have another close friend who likes to buy specialty sneakers and shoes. He owns more than sixty pairs, all different colors, patterns, and styles, and they range in price from eighty dollars to two hundred dollars. He even has two pairs of self-lacing shoes (don't ask me how much they cost; you don't want to know). To some people, even myself at times, these price points seem crazy and outlandish. I hear about specialty sneakers and his latest pair and I think, '*I could never spend that on a pair of shoes.*'

But his money is his money. He can spend it how he wants to. His perspective on his spending is different than mine. It's not my place to judge. (And it doesn't serve me to judge.) Maybe he doesn't understand why I own so many coffee mugs. That's okay, too.

The same goes for you. Your money, your choices, and your perspectives are your own.

I'm not saying we can buy every single thing we want. We don't always get to have and do whatever brings us joy (especially at the risk of costing us our financial progress and success). I can't spend all my money because I say it brings value to me, not without getting caught up in debt or living paycheck-to-paycheck.

But I do weigh my expenses against one another when I need perspective, and I try to think in terms of hours worked or days traded for income, instead of just dollars and cents. For example, one day of work pays for our entire month's Internet and then some. Suddenly, that Internet plan doesn't seem so costly. But if getting my hair colored requires two days of work, I might rethink my values and how I trade that money.

Think about the value of your money. Let this help you discover, develop, or change your perspectives on spending.

Remember, there is no "good" or "bad" spending. And the amounts of money we spend, just like what we earn, is relative.

Every person lives a different life in a different situation.

Jason would rather buy a new video game than pay for that dinner out (and they cost the same thing). His preferences are not good or bad; they're just his own. And when he hesitates to spend the money, I remind him of these perspectives. Sometimes we spend forty dollars on brunch and the next day I wonder if I'm being too frivolous with paying for organic produce. I have to remind myself about the perspectives.

No, adopting a new perspective won't happen overnight. Yes, it's a lifelong learning process.

But it definitely beats working seventy hours in cheap, crappy shoes.

it's all relative

I've mentioned more than a few times how much extra we worked to pull this off in the timeline that we did.

But let me be clear: Working extra and making extra money did NOT automatically guarantee we would handle that money appropriately and pay off the debt.

Income amounts are relative. What is a high income for one person is a low income for another; the same goes for a low income being another person's highest income. (And if you think about it, the terms 'low income' and 'high income' are relative, too.) My record year of income could be your lowest year. The hourly wage someone worked toward for years might be the wage another person started with.

The most important part of personal finances and getting out of debt is *not* how much money you make.

What matters the most is how you *handle* the money.

I could earn forty thousand dollars a year and spend forty thousand dollars a year. I could increase my income to fifty thousand and spend fifty thousand. On the flipside, I could make thirty thousand and set aside ten thousand for debt.

In all three scenarios, the amount of income didn't promise the amount of debt paid off.

Making more money does not guarantee any debt repayment or savings contribution *unless you commit and decide* to put that extra income toward your goals.

I've heard a lot of reasons someone "can't" do what we did. *"I couldn't work that many hours." "I don't make that much money."*

So start where you are and with what you have. Focus on handling the income you currently bring in. Decide what to do with it before it hits your bank account and then *stick to your plan.*

Take care of your bills, feed yourself and others living in your home, pay minimum monthly payments on other debts, and then become intentional with where you put the leftover money.

Put it to your goals, whatever they are. If your goal is to save, save. If your goal is to pay off debt, put it to debt. If you want to give it away, give it away!

But don't tell me you can't do something like we did because you believe you don't make enough money.

I'm not telling you to clock sixteen-hour days. I'm telling you to appropriately handle *any* amount of money you have. In this case it will pay off to work smarter instead of just harder.

If you do these things and you still don't have the income you desire, look at what you can change in the equation. Can you work more? Can you pick up or create a second job for a small amount of time? Can you earn a raise at work or bring in extra cash off commissions?

I myself have never worked anything but hourly jobs, so my first instinct was to pick up more hours and as much overtime as possible. Do I wish I could have made the amount I did without logging so many hours? You bet. But it wasn't possible at the time, so I did what I had to do.

We make time for a lot of experiences and things that we value. We make sure we're home in time for "the game," we set aside money for Christmas, we take a yearly vacation, we watch TV, read books, play games, shop, go out for dinner or drinking, and attend concerts.

None of these things are negative or underserving of your time. But also make time for your goal and desire of taking control of your money.

Own your life, accept responsibility for your time, and tell yourself a new story: this part of life is more important than the others.

For me, becoming debt-free was more important than X amount of hours of TV or leisure time on my phone. Setting aside time to budget was more valuable than rereading my favorite book.

Just like income, time is relative.

You can have all the extra hours the genie will grant you; it's how you spend them that matters.

And, speaking of income, on that note...

you are worth more than your income

This is a little outside of our debt-free story, but it's a topic that has haunted me since I began working when I was sixteen.

I've told you more than a few times that I love talking and learning about money. A person doesn't have to be an expert in something to thrive in that space, and this is one of my spaces.

But my mindset toward my own income has not always been positive.

Money means a lot of things to us. To some, money is stressful, unattainable, or inconsequential. To me, money is freedom to choose, access to the world and personal possessions, a way to give to another person, and more.

In the past it's also been a status symbol. Making more money was always better and more desirable. So, naturally, making less money was less desirable. I never wanted to become an adult and *not* earn what I believed was a decent income (again, it's all relative).

But sometimes we tie the amount of money we make to our self-worth, and this mindset has not positively served me. Instead it's made me feel stressed out, inferior, and embarrassed.

I've judged myself against others based on our incomes, our job titles, or our ages. *Twenty-six and still serving coffee? Twenty-six and only making X amount?* And later on, once my hours were cut back and the overtime was gone, these thoughts and feelings only increased.

I didn't realize how much I tied the income to my worth until the income dropped and progress with our next financial goal slowed down.

Allowing our income to inform and influence what we think of our worth is damaging. It's hard to clock in at work day after day if you believe the amount you're being paid suggests that you are less worthy of a person, or that other aspects of your life don't matter. It's too tempting to chase a higher paycheck with hopes and expectations that this number will increase our value and our self-esteem.

When this number is the lens we use to view ourselves, all of the other definitions and qualities of our person and worth fall away and seem irrelevant. We are likely to question our talents and passions and the attributes that contribute to the world and create fulfillment.

It's also important that we are mindful and committed to treating people equally, and that we don't regard them as inferior based on their income, or whether they have one or not.

We are all worth more than our income.

I know it's easier to read than to believe – trust me, I'm still working on it.

I wish I had addressed this issue in myself before becoming debt-free, because becoming debt-free was not the whole-hearted celebration I wanted it to be. It was bittersweet; I associated a lot of the person I am to that goal and the income that helped get us there.

But I am worth more than my income, and my life is more important than the money I use to fund it.

sacrifice...but don't suffer

"So, let me get this straight. No vacations; no eating out; no buying new clothes; barely any new personal items; no expensive gifts; no wedding anniversary celebrations; no extra holidays; only generic brands; less sleep; less leisure time; and hours and hours of extra work?"

Yep, sounds about right.

"You poor things! It must be so hard and it sounds terrible! Sounds like..."

Like suffering?

At first it does. At first it looks miserable. But it's really not.

We didn't look at it as suffering. Instead, we saw it for what it truly was: sacrificing. Sacrifice Now, so we don't have to Later. Say 'No' Now, so we can say 'Yes' After.

But the line between sacrifice and suffer is thin. We toed it often when we weren't careful. (I say 'we' but we all know it was really just me. Ninety-five hours, remember?) I got too close to the line when I worked more hours than I knew were healthy. I edged my way around it when I mentally bullied myself for not finding more ways and hours to make money from home.

At times I didn't take care of myself as well as I could have. Or I put off buying items that would sustain my schedule and wellness. I forgot to eat often or kept working through the hunger pangs. I drank more coffee and caffeinated beverages than I knew were wise. (I worked at a *coffee* bar, after all.) I wore out many pairs of work shoes, but at the cost of foot problems and potential injuries that could been avoided if I'd just bought a new pair when I needed it.

But we were doing something epic! I was on a noble journey! There wasn't time for self-care! The dollars had to go to my loans, not to *more* shoes (and socks, when the toe holes appeared, of course).

Slowing down would be weak. Doing "less" would make this take longer. Success had to be early mornings and late nights, caffeine jitters and forgotten meals and go-go-go because stopping wasn't an option.

But then success started to look and feel like suffering.

(I was "fine," though. Near the end I'd spent almost two years doing this, so there was nothing to be concerned about...right?)

You can assume I was wrong.

Success that led to suffering was not the same as sacrifice.

Getting to the finish line wasn't success if I lost a limb (or two) during the race. I had to push myself back behind that line.

I had to learn something crucial, that thing some of us hate to hear about but we're all searching for and struggling to keep if we find it or create it: balance.

I would not find balance in suffering. It could only be sustained in a time of careful sacrifice.

I don't regret the amount I worked. I *do* regret not taking care of myself sooner. It wasn't until the last nine months that I really defined our differences between sacrificing and suffering.

Some of the differences looked like: buying new and better shoes sooner; investing in wellness tools that would prevent us from getting sick or worn down (such as antibiotics *before* a flu ran its course); choosing healthier foods despite a higher price tag; and, most important of all, accepting that we really were doing the best and most that we could.

Your mental and physical health should not be at risk for the sake of attacking debt or repairing your personal finances. I know that we glorify late nights followed by early mornings and stretching ourselves so thin we snap without warning. I know that so much of life feels like a competition. I know how it feels to be driven by guilt and shame instead of encouragement and reassurance that things will be okay.

I don't want you to read this book and set out to beat our timeline or top my personal record for how many hours I worked in a week (it's ninety-eight; seriously, don't do it). I don't want you to cut down your grocery budget so much that you skip a meal or eat crappy food to save money.

You need to be physically and mentally healthy and safe more than you *ever* need to pay off a credit card or fund a retirement account. When you have the flu and you think you might pass out at work and the doctor says you shouldn't have worked that fourteen-hour day, sleep is more important than overtime.

If you set out to achieve any money goal and you find yourself sick with anxiety and fear and you can't escape the pressure you've put on yourself, please ask for professional help. Talk to a mental health counselor. Hire a financial advisor to teach you whatever you're struggling to learn.

Be kind to yourself. It's worth more than you know.

we all have choices

I've told you how difficult it was. The hours, the pain, the guilt, the claustrophobic feelings. It wasn't a walk in the park. We didn't want to do what we were doing. My days were consumed by this obsession, by my need for us to be debt-free and financially free.

But maybe there's still a part of you that thinks we had it easy. Or that we have some magical stuff flowing in our veins that made what we did possible. I've heard it all: we don't have kids, we "only" owed student loans, we had opportunity for more income, we agreed on money as a couple, we were able to focus (and the list goes on).

Honestly, I don't think any of the people with those comments were actually concerned about what they said.

I think it all comes down to choices.

We chose to make extra money, not spend it, and pay off our debt. We chose not to take vacations or eat in restaurants often. We chose to budget carefully and spend intentionally. We chose to learn from our mistakes. We chose to get rid of material possessions we didn't need. We chose to focus on this goal until it was completed. We chose to work together. We chose to sacrifice. We chose financial freedom.

As I said before, we sign up for each expense, for every dollar we spend. We choose where we live, what we eat, what we wear, what entertainment subscriptions we use, which phone company to pay, and the car we drive (we even choose to what extent we insure it).

Life does happen at times, but, for the most part, we are wholly responsible for our personal finances (and the consequences).

The budget is not a binding contract. It is a written reflection of how we choose to live our lives, and we get to decide what this reflection looks like.

We all have choices. That's the reality of what we did and what you can do.

Trust me when I say I understand that you don't want to do this. Neither did I. It was hard not to buy clothing I wanted. It was hard to pass up high quality coffee and expensive brunches and new books and video games and weekend trips to visit friends in Boston. Maybe it sounds like we did this all with ease, but that is not the case.

Imagine for a moment: you earned an extra five hundred dollars this week, or you brought home an extra four thousand dollars this month. You could pay for a vacation TODAY. You could buy that new whatever and it wouldn't hurt your bank account. You could save for two months and buy a new car and stop worrying about the sad, dying box on wheels you keep saving from the junkyard.

It would be so nice and feel so great. Then the next month you could do the same thing!

And that debt, those loans...I mean, you'll get to them one day, right? What's another month (or six)?

That scenario involves a lot of choices. We faced those choices every week and every month. We had that extra income and we could have spent it all. We could have taken multiple trips (assuming I would take off work). We could have put off the debt by a month (or six, or twelve, or forever) and rationalized every choice we made.

But we chose differently. You know what we did instead. You know we said No until we could freely say Yes.

That's the only important difference between us and anyone who chooses differently.

The only drawback about having choices is when the fact of having choices at all makes it more difficult to make a decision.

We're concerned with making the "right" choice, choosing the "correct" way and answer. We want the "best" route and oftentimes the easiest or cheapest option. We don't want to do research to figure out what foods are best for us and then make a meal plan; we just want the right answer to be set in front of us with a fork and a knife.

Sometimes it feels it would be easier to have one brand, one method, and one option to rely on and default to. Instead we have twenty kinds of ketchup and fifty brands of clothing for the same type of shirt, and hundreds of different books on fixing our money problems and a rising wave of voices shouting, "THIS IS THE BEST ONE," and "You're missing out if you don't pick THIS one."

And you know it only gets more complicated than that.

Don't be afraid to make your choices. And don't be intimidated by the number of possibilities or the risk of failure. Not choosing, and instead blindly pointing and hoping, is worse than making the "wrong" choice.

If you feel you've messed up with your choices in the past, I have great news: you can choose differently now! You can pick another option, method, plan, resource, and direction.

You can pick different car insurance, a cheaper Internet plan, a bank account without fees, a budgeting method that you love and that you don't dread, and a plan for your money that makes sense to you and motivates you.

A lot of us are facing these same dilemmas. But our choices decide our future, and it's crucial that we create this future.

Jason and I don't have anything supernatural in our veins or more "self-discipline," or less want for what money can buy. (Minimalism helped with this, but I still want to take trips that cost a lot more than a new book.)

We don't have a perfect way that guarantees our choices are the best or right ones. We make the best choice we can and we fix it later if we have to.

You have the same choices and probably similar opportunities.

Work with what you've got instead of putting thought and energy into what you don't have. Take responsibility for the choices that brought you to this situation and then make choices that will lead you out of it.

I hated being at fault for my mess. I hated that I could have done things differently and avoided the years of intensity and struggle. But I reached a point where I had to accept the fault and embrace my responsibility to make choices.

I had to *choose* to choose better.

believe that what you do is important

We were sitting at a friend's wedding reception (we attended quite a few weddings during this time), surrounded by a lot of people we didn't know. My social anxiety was rising.

Small talk makes me uncomfortable and I'm terrible at bonding with strangers. It's tough to find common ground, and that's without the easy trappings of comparison and insecurity.

The reception progressed. I tried to ease into casual conversation. *(Oh, you know the groom? We know the bride...you know so-and-so, too? Wow, it's a small world...)* Then the conversation turned toward a common topic: *What do you do?*

This topic was easy for me. I can talk about work and industries of trade and business all day long. Whatever your line of work is, I guarantee I'm interested. Tell me how you make your income, what your degree or schooling is, and what your next move might be.

But please, please don't ask me in return.

Why? Because of a lot of reasons.

Because I'm not using my degree(s). Because I'm not always doing something I find particularly stimulating or meaningful. Because it doesn't pay a lot without excessive overtime, because I spend a lot of my time at work wishing for something else...

I sat at the reception that day and listened to our tablemates speak about what they are doing with their lives for income, hobby, and leisure. I was fascinated with their purpose and the charitable causes and companies they were working for. They were each doing something important, meaningful, stimulating, and even with decent pay.

I could feel my self-worth and appreciation faltering. I felt inferior and became startled by how unhappy and unfulfilled I was.

I left the reception troubled and mentally unprepared for the next day. Back to Monday, back to my unfulfilling work and time, and I felt there was nothing I could do to fix or stop it. I was working where and the amount I was because of the debt. I had to finish this ultimate goal and mission before I could move on to the Next Big Thing.

But the end wasn't here yet. We still had a few months until the debt would be paid off, and many months after *that* until we completed our next financial goal. These personal missions were too important to me to shirk financial responsibility or risk losing my current income.

I had worked this way and this much for so long without an issue that affected me this negatively. But I suddenly couldn't fathom going to work the next day with these escalating feelings and a damaged mindset. But I would have to do it anyway. I would have to keep going. The end was in sight but I still had work to do to get there.

Doing the same type of work day in and day out can become frustrating. Feeling like a hamster on a wheel undermined the motivation I had when we first started. I knew when we would meet our goals and knew it would be worth it, but we still had to log all the working hours to make it happen.

Days turned into weeks and weeks turned into months. Time passes very quickly in hindsight, but in the middle of a process like this it's the day-to-day that can be discouraging and hard to trek through.

I worked through most weeks without a problem. The body and mind can adapt to almost any situation, including the grueling work schedules we endured. But some moments were tough, especially near the end.

My job was primarily customer service, which is not always a picnic (or any other fun type of event). The routine can grow monotonous, the same people say and do the same things (good or bad), the grind doesn't change, and the minutes begin to pass slower...and slower...

At times I was miserable. And being miserable only made me more miserable. Progress with the loans was now an expected standard, no longer a thrilling prospect to work toward. Seeing the light at the end of the tunnel just made me dread the rest of the tunnel. I became bored, irritable, and "over it."

Some days I didn't think I could stand another second of what I was doing (let alone a few more months). Everything hurt; sleeping was difficult; my mind was consumed by the dread and tedium; my patience was waning.

I needed to feel awake and alive again. I needed to feel like what I was doing mattered beyond meeting our goal of becoming debt-free.

But those conversations at the reception put something into my mind that hadn't been there before. It was more powerful than the boredom or the physical pain. It was too critical to ignore.

I didn't find meaning or purpose in the work I was doing.

I was making money and achieving a goal, but that wasn't enough. I had been presented with something other people had that I did not, and now I needed it more than anything.

Believe that what you do is important.

That's what I needed to do. I needed to think beyond myself, beyond my negativity, and focus on a bigger picture. Doing the work for one goal and one person (myself) wasn't enough anymore. It didn't feel like it mattered.

I had to change this mindset.

Every job comes with its own form of repetitiveness and potential dread, even the most fascinating dream job I can think of. And while this particular job was not going to be permanent for me, some of our jobs or lines of work will be. Let's face it: the grass isn't greener on the other side, so it is time we water the garden (or desert, let's be honest) we've got.

Believe that what you do is important. Believe it at work, at home, with your finances, your relationships, your plans and goals, your interests, and anywhere else you give your energy and time.

I made coffee for a living while getting out of debt. To me, it served only that purpose. It provided the income and overtime I needed to meet this huge goal and to produce changes in my life.

But to someone else, my work didn't do those things. Instead, it served them in other ways. I gave them coffee; I helped provide them with food; I smiled when they were having good days and bad days; I listened to their stories and told some of my own. I took care of someone aside from myself. I served a purpose beyond the one I could see.

It's been a difficult mindset to cultivate, but I do believe the work I did (and still do) is important. That's what kept me going in the last few months. Now debt-free, it still keeps me going.

No matter what your line of work is, what you are doing is important.

I know we tend to place more importance and prominence on certain jobs and fields of work over others; it's inevitable. But we all contribute and we all benefit from our individual and shared work. We are all someone's customer, client, or patient; a lot of us are managing people, departments, and corporations; many do the work that "nobody wants to do"; and some of us do the specialized work that only a few can do.

All of it is important. If you are not in the work force, your non-paid work is important. If you volunteer, your work is important.

It's time we believe it and believe our work is intended for more than a paycheck.

Do not fear the burden of or desire for purpose. Embrace it.

soft landings

Sometimes working as much as I did felt like being on a perpetual high, like flying. We were making so much progress and at breakneck speeds. Each individual loan we paid off brought us to another planet, closer and closer to the stars. We hit turbulence a few times, but the rest of the time felt weightless.

We were doing this. We could do anything.

But could I slow down?

Around the same time that I confronted and corrected the suffering versus sacrifice, nine months before we were finished, I felt a shift in my capabilities. I *could* keep going with the schedule I had...or could I? And if I really could, did that mean I should?

I began to experience intense foot pain daily. I had stressful dreams about waking up and not being able to walk. I was reluctant to complete other normal adult-related tasks, like grocery shopping and attending social events that required standing. I had to wear compression socks in other shoes, buy yet another pair of work shoes, soak my feet daily, and be careful not to strain them if I exercised.

I worried that I permanently damaged them with my schedule and the long period of time without quality shoes. (If you're on the edge of your seat wondering about my foot issues, at this time of writing I've found a special massager that helps with blood flow, leg cramps, and plantar fasciitis.)

I was incredibly frustrated by this physical limitation. I criticized myself for letting it happen and for not being "stronger" and able to keep going. *How dare my feet let me down after I subjected them to borderline inhumane working conditions and abnormal hours of usage?* (Please roll your eyes with me.)

But dwelling on this negativity would not help. My feet wouldn't magically feel better.

In my experience, much of what we're dealing with is brought on by our own decisions and actions. That thought could be applied to our debt and my working conditions. I chose to work this much, after all. I could easily choose *not* to work this much. I was the only person forcing this schedule and intensity.

I didn't know if I could slow down, but with this pain and these circumstances now it seemed I didn't have a choice. (My idea of slowing down was working sixty hours instead of seventy-five, but I digress.)

Then, as if something or someone in the universe heard me and doubted my ability to make that choice, the decision was made for me. The dilemma was taken out of my hands: I was losing some of my overtime. Not all of it (not yet), but half of it.

At first I resisted the opportunity to view this as a good and necessary change. I was too determined to pay off our debt by a certain time (August, instead of December), but I knew this deadline was possible only because of my current overtime situation.

I feared my own pressure and expectations. I feared being viewed as less of a hard worker if I didn't work as many hours. But the decision was made and I had to accept it.

This was the beginning of my soft landing into becoming debt-free. I regained some sleep, ate more meals, had a day off every two weeks, and started to recover from the foot pain. I adjusted my expectations and rationalized with my mindset to offset the pressure.

Soft landings are important. It's good to feel and know we are capable, but this shouldn't be tested at the cost of our health and sanity. I love the obsession and giving my all, but I'm not immune to limitations.

These limitations do not limit our worth, our abilities, or our opportunities. They just limit the ways we can torment ourselves with undue burdens and stress.

And since I'm on a pun kick in this book: Even the pilot best at flying still needs to know how to safely land the plane.

making time for what's important
(sacrificing the sacrifice)

In the midst of our debt-free struggles and successes, we sacrificed a lot...including our time.

Putting spending and vacations and savings on hold felt logical. But time with each other, time with our friends and families, and time spent leisurely were harder sacrifices to make.

It was our hope that all of those things would be waiting for us when we emerged from our months and years of all work and little play. After all, I could read that new book down the road. We could buy the better couch when this was completed. We saw each other everyday, just not as much as we would in the future. And our friends and families understood.

But I always wondered: where do we draw the line? When would it better serve us to say no to an extra shift and say yes to an extra family gathering? And what if something happened and we missed it, or missed out on something important because of our sacrifice?

I personally rarely drew the line. I sacrificed almost all of my time with loved ones in favor of making this goal happen as quickly as possible.

It wasn't until six months after we became debt-free that I regretted this decision.

We can never know what the future holds. Today is what we're looking at, but I'd be lying if I said I'm not always thinking about tomorrow, too. We have confidence there will always be a tomorrow for us.

I had this confidence when I took on all the extra work. But I underestimated how much time I was sacrificing. I neglected to remember that we can save money and pay off debt, but we cannot reclaim or create time.

My grandfather died six months after we became debt-free. We did see him more during those six months, but not as much as we could have. Not as much as *I* could have. But during those two (almost three) years, I didn't visit as often, didn't attend every family dinner, and kept telling myself there would be more time.

You know as well as I do that I was wrong.

This sacrifice of time (not just with my grandparents, but with everyone important to me) is my only regret for how we became debt-free. I pushed myself to become debt-free faster so that we could get back to a normal schedule sooner, but maybe I should have paused more often and used the time while I had it.

I don't tell you this to scare you, or to make you worry you're missing out on life or that someone will die or you'll have regret from becoming debt-free. I tell it as a gentle reminder to make time for what is important, even during this intense goal-oriented stage.

Becoming debt-free is important. Focusing on personal finances is vital to a secure future and the Tomorrow we dream about and have confidence in.

But there are things in life we may only have for today.

If you fear this sacrifice of time, it's even more reason to stay focused on and determined about your goals.

Use extra time you have to give energy to what's most significant, whether it's social life, family time, leisure enjoyment, or something else you value. I can get trapped in the vortex of Instagram and Hulu and other time-sucking activities if I don't call myself out on it and keep aligned to my goals.

How many times did this happen while I was working to be debt-free? And how much of that time could have been spent with my grandparents or to have dinner with a close friend instead?

Unlike money, I know I can't make time. *But* just like with money, I can control how I spend it.

I know my grandpa knew why we weren't around as much. I know he was proud of what we did and how we did it. I know he didn't begrudge our absence or find fault in our sacrifice. But if I could go back and do it differently, I would. If I could say no to a shift and spend the time with him, I would.

I dedicated this book to our parents, but I dedicate my work ethic and discipline to succeed to him. Truly, without him, this entire story wouldn't be possible.

the other side

We became debt-free on December 7, 2018.

I went to work at five a.m., looked at our mobile banking to see that our paychecks went in, clicked the app to make our final payment to the debt, and posted the update to Instagram and Facebook. Then I continued with my workday, and I can't remember any other significant details.

I want to tell you that it was an incredible, noteworthy, and remarkable day. That the sun shone brighter, my step had pep, customers were nicer, figurative weights lifted from my back, and all was well within my corner of the world.

But it didn't happen like that. That Friday was like most other Fridays. Honestly, it was a little flat and didn't feel as meaningful as some other payment days had felt.

This was supposed to be THE BIG DAY: THE DAY TO CHANGE EVERYTHING. Something magical was supposed to happen. We should have a thrown a party, erected a monument, torched our old debt-free tracking papers, printed and shredded my student loan records...

Becoming debt-free did not fix our lives. It changed our lives, but did not fix them.

I was still miserable at my job. I was still pining for another type of work and another type of life. I wanted to make more money without having to work crazy amounts of overtime. I wanted to experience financial success without pinching pennies so hard my thumbs became sore.

We wanted to enjoy our money in ways we hadn't for nearly four years, maybe for our whole lives, but we felt obligated to What Was Next.

We still had financial goals we planned to tackle after this and knew it would take more discipline and sacrifice.

Becoming debt-free WAS a big deal to me. I did feel the rush of adrenaline as I was posting that update. Throughout the day I kept reminding myself, *we are debt-free; we are debt-free; we don't owe anything to anybody; we are done.*

But I wanted to feel the way everyone expected me to feel. I wanted the freedom to wash over me in waves, but instead it ebbed and flowed. I wanted to feel the relief I had been sure would come to me.

I realize now that this freedom and relief would come later, over time.

But until that happened, we still had life to live and things to do. We wanted to save for a large emergency fund, restart retirement contribution, donate to a new charity, and a whole list of goals I had written down.

These goals were exactly like the debt-free goal: we would have to work hard, save intentionally, budget smartly, and stay focused. Life would be more or less the same, but now we could take fuller, deeper breaths and cross this item off our financial to-do list.

The other side of this journey is not paradise. It's an amazing feeling and experience, and I will always be grateful those intense and extreme days are behind us. But not every life change is a life hack. Our financial future is brighter and more secure, but we still have to put in effort to make it happen.

Being debt-free is not our final destination.

It is our new way of life.

facing the fear of spending money

Can you picture walking into a store or restaurant and picking out and buying any single item you want without looking at the price tag? Without even glancing at the bill?

Can you imagine leaving more than a twenty-percent tip, maybe thirty or forty percent, and not second-guessing the decision?

What about picking up a gift for someone and not feeling cheap or embarrassed because they deserve so much more than what you can offer?

I dreamed of doing these things. I felt motivated by picturing myself doing them because it felt *good.* It made me feel *free.*

Of course I wanted to become debt-free so we could save money and invest for our future, but come on; who doesn't think about what it will feel like to freely spend money? Who doesn't fantasize about taking a vacation they don't have to tightly budget?

But I was not aware that I would have to alter the way my brain was trained to look at the act of spending money. I was not prepared for the next mental shift I would have to make. I didn't realize my habits were so ingrained that it would be a challenge to do anything differently.

I had to relearn how to spend money without feeling guilty. I had to acknowledge and deal with my fear surrounding spending money.

When we were paying the debt, I opened my mind beyond the scarcity mindset. I accepted the abundance of income we could create and taught my mind to view the debt as an obstacle to overcome rather than an undefeatable enemy.

But I also coached myself not to spend or overspend needlessly. I shied away from Instagram product ads, online sales, meals outside of my apartment and work place, and coffee I didn't make myself. I embraced minimalism and dealt with FOMO. Not buying an iced coffee each day wasn't what paid off my debt. It was my mindset *behind* not buying the iced coffee, the book, the shirt, the thirteenth day planner I was *never* going to use.

Becoming debt-free should have also freed me from these financial and mental barriers.

But I have to tell the truth: the thought of freely spending money again terrified me. I felt panicky at the thought of getting caught up in old spending patterns, the patterns and habits that made it easy to go into debt (and stay in debt).

I now viewed each dollar more critically than before.

It's interesting; you would have thought these would have been my feelings and fears while we paid off our debt, but it was the opposite. I trained and trusted myself to make clear, goal-oriented spending decisions. I spent money when we had to, but didn't experience regret.

But now, faced with the new reality of freed income and one hundred thousand dollars of debt behind me, I was afraid to part with our money.

I wanted to quit my current job, but I knew I needed the security of a larger emergency fund before I could do this in good conscience. I began to develop odd, fidgety habits with our income and expenses. I checked our bank accounts obsessively, running numbers in my head over and over again, trying to figure out when this quitting would be possible.

I hesitated over each item we bought, each meal we ate out, even holiday costs and gifts we had already budgeted for. I dreaded larger future expenses that awaited us (as if the dread would help) and wrung my hands over the coming tax bill. I bought a new book for seven dollars and then considered returning it because I felt so guilty...I didn't *need* that book. But I needed to quit my job. *Where were my priorities now?*

My mind was flooded with worry and constructed of revolving doors of guilt and shame and numbers and dollar signs. I went through one door only to go through another. I mentally beat myself senseless trying to figure out what was happening.

Where was the freedom I promised myself? What happened to the reasons we became debt-free?

Did I become debt-free only to hyperventilate at the thought of spending a thousand dollars on a new mattress we desperately needed? The mattress we put off for five years because we wanted to be debt-free when we purchased it? Did I become debt-free to consider cashing in change jars to pay for groceries, instead of using money from our paychecks, because I was afraid to spend the funds?

Did I become debt-free to put myself into another mental prison?

You know the answer. It's a resounding NO.

I became debt-free to be FREE.

Free of the debt hanging over my head, the scarcity mindset plaguing my sleep, the discomfort of forever wanting and never having. Free of the worry of not having enough. Free of the fear of spending money.

I had never felt this particular fear before. Where did it come from? And why, after this intense period of time, was I feeling it? Why *now*, when that time was over?

My gut told me that it was because of all we had done to pay off our loans. We had made more money than ever before, and, technically speaking, now it was gone. It was never ours to claim and we didn't become attached to it. We relied on it and expected it, but we knew we'd already "spent" it. There was no reason to fear what could happen to this money.

But the money we made after this was over...that was a different story. That money was free for us to keep and give and spend.

This should have been exhilarating.

But my past decisions haunted me. In the past I'd had the same opportunity with money I earned, and I wasn't smart with it. I went into debt, overspent on materialistic desires and unfulfilling items, and did not save a single dollar unless I had a short-term goal for it.

If that was my past, and if I hadn't done anything differently until I had no other sustainable choice, what was stopping me from returning to my old habits? How could I know I had legitimately grown and learned from those mistakes? Where was the line between who I had been financially and who I wanted to be?

Just like with the purpose of a successful budget (choosing where money goes) and a foolproof plan to become debt-free (handling money intentionally from a healthy money mindset), I had to decide to draw the line. I had to choose to permanently change and grow. Becoming debt-free would not do this for me (because it's not a fix-all, remember?).

People can always go back into debt. I see it all the time. We pay off a credit card and max out a new one. We pay off a car loan and take on another financing plan. Or we get a paycheck ahead and then celebrate too much and fall back into the patterns that barely tread water.

I knew we would never go back into debt. If nothing else, going through this has stomped out all desire to ever make another payment...on anything. But I knew it was possible to remain debt-free and still have nothing to show for it. I know a person can be debt-free but still live paycheck to paycheck, consuming all they bring in.

I did not want that to be our story. My new habits needed to stick.

It was not enough to make money and not go into debt. We needed to keep this money and make it work for us for savings, investing, giving, and funding retirement.

When I consider all of this, it makes sense that I was afraid to spend it. With this success behind (and now defining) us, and with equally important goals ahead, it's natural that I would fear spending money.

But I couldn't sit in the fear for too long. I did not break out of one mental prison to willfully step into another.

I went back to the basics: money in and money out. No emotions, no baggage, and no narratives.

Money doesn't have power. What we do with it is the power (either that is held over us, or that we wield). Money should not cause fear. It is our actions with it that cause fear. I could control those actions. I could control what I did with our money.

And in declaring that, I realized that I wasn't facing fear of spending money. I was facing fear of myself.

The only way to combat this fear was to remind myself of where I was and how far I had come. I had to look back on what we did that was good and trust that we could keep going in this new direction.

We took responsibility, embraced minimalism, addressed FOMO, stuck to a solid plan for three years, and we loved the results and the way it felt to live like this.

There's always a time in life where we need to start looking forward and resist the urge to look back.

For me, that time was now.

dave, tony, warren, grant, monica, jason, and you

Becoming debt-free has been the most rewarding and amazing experience of our lives (besides getting married, of course).

But for me personally it's also been the most humbling.

Remember in the beginning when I thought I knew everything and was arrogant enough to think I could get by and succeed without the rest? Obviously I was wrong, and I'm glad I found that out. If I hadn't, we might still be back in that movie theater swiping over-drafted debit cards for popcorn and candy.

I learned new ways to think about and handle money and opened my eyes and mind to a lot of resources, many of them contradictory and teaching different ideas and methods.

At first this contradiction paralyzed me. I was torn between information that was solid, and opposing information that also seemed solid. I wanted to do it the "best" way and the fastest way. But what if I took the wrong advice?

Dave said to do it like this...but Suze said actually do it like that...Grant didn't agree with either one...Tony didn't say anything that any of them said so far...and Warren Buffet is just Warren-freaking-Buffet.

What would they think if I didn't follow their lead?

If you've read this book or others like it, or if you've skimmed some blogs or listened to a podcast and you're overwhelmed and feeling pulled in too many directions, I offer you this (yes, in addition to all of that): there is no "wrong" way to get out of debt.

Personal finances are important, but there isn't a morality clause involved. Remember: what you do with your money is your choice. It is *your* money and life.

Frankly, it isn't my business and it doesn't affect me at all. Do I want you to experience the hope and success that we have? Of course I do. But I'm never going to say you have to do it exactly how we did it to make it happen.

Just start where you are.

Do what makes common sense to you.

Be open to trying different methods and adopting a new mindset or perception, but don't let the opinions of other resources and people give you anxiety that leaves you paralyzed like I was.

Take it slow if you have to. Focus on your small steps if the large leaps are overwhelming.

Be deliberate with your time and your energy: only give it to what fills and sustains you.

What was doable for us may not be for you. Honestly, a lot of people make more money in forty hours than I could make in eighty. This doesn't mean they are required to pick up another forty hours to speed up their process.

Would I have done that myself? Of course! I'm an obsessed workaholic! But that doesn't mean you have to be. Maybe that person just needs to change their spending habits or look more closely at their expenses.

Our lives are all different; it would only make sense that our processes and timelines would be as well.

We're not competing against one another.

Don't sell yourself short. A lot of people looked at us and said they admired what we did but they could never do it themselves. The one thing I always wanted to say (but never did) was, "Well...have you tried?"

Are you selling yourself short? Do you doubt your capabilities and willingness to succeed?

We all tell ourselves stories about our lives and who we are. And not all of these stories lead to happy, successful endings.

Jason and I decided to tell each other and ourselves that we could do this. We could work and sacrifice more than ever and then be done. We'd never have to do this again.

We've got one life: why not go at it with all you've got? What have you got to lose?

We all look up to people who have achieved a greatness we'd like to experience. These are people we can learn from and hopefully relate to.

But don't put yourself below them or believe you are inferior to them. A lot of people have done things I'll never do, or things I want to but haven't yet. I am not less because of that. They are not superior to me because of that.

Remember rule one? Do not compare yourself to us. Do not compare yourself to anyone else, either. Your personal finances are just as important (and just as powerful!) as mine. Your success is just as attainable as ours has been.

You are no less capable or qualified than we are. Not finance experts, remember? We work in customer service and concrete production plants, live in a two-bedroom apartment with our cat, and we are in love with the life we've created.

You can be too.

Become your own inspiration, someone you'd look up to and want to learn from. I prefer to learn from the person who has actually done what they're teaching. For example, I'm not going to tell you how to prepare your taxes on your own because I don't do that.

But I can tell you how to get out of debt and feel the freedom I feel. And if you are willing to do the work and dedicate yourself to this goal, one day you can, too.

the end (or just the beginning?)

At the time of this writing we have been debt-free for ten months.

In that time I've left my full-time job. (Yes, you read that correctly: the "debt-free girl" who worked all that overtime and was obsessed with income has decided it's time to take a break from that life.)

I kept telling myself that all those hours and my increasing misery were serving a purpose, and that when the purpose was fulfilled I could free myself of that obligation.

But once the purpose was served this was much easier thought than put into action. I grew accustomed to a certain income level and the expectation of working so many extra hours.

I began to question: who am I without this debt-free goal? What is my life without the one-hundred-day work stretches and being exhausted from being on my feet all the time?

I was forced to figure this out when my overtime was completely cut and my motivation to keep doing what I was doing rapidly disappeared.

I had two choices: stay with this current path and begin to juggle parts of my life again; or wave one of my white flags (and possibly surrender my main source of income) and focus on what I wanted to do next.

This seems like an easy decision to make, but it wasn't. I was comfortable where I was, even if I wanted to be somewhere different. I had a guaranteed base income and schedule. Everything surrounding me was familiar.

But a part of me hated it. I was ready to move on. These two sides waged war in my mind each morning I woke up and each night I went to sleep.

Moving on would be startling and difficult. Doing something new (for income or otherwise) was intimidating and would take time.

I had never done this before. I had never made a financial decision without first feeling backed into a corner. I went to college because I thought I had to. I took on debt because I didn't know there was another way. I chased degrees to provide meaning, which at times felt more important than income. I picked up a new job to pay off the debt. I worked myself until burnout to become...

Free.

That's why we did it, right?

We sacrificed and pushed and said No and put everything on hold to pay off the debt, yes...but more than that, to become financially free.

This really was my choice. There wasn't a financial burden. No expectations. Zero pressure.

Just me and my head and my gut and a question: what next?

I made my choice and it was both easy and hard. It was bittersweet, but it felt right. I made this decision for the right reasons. I decided to be who I want to be and do what I want to do without being tied to and held down by financial burdens and goals.

No, I've never done that before.

But that's why we did this.

We did this so that we could choose our lives. Life doesn't happen to us anymore. Debt is not our master. Money is not the focal point of our present or our future.

About the work decision: I decided to move on. Soon after that I also left my part-time job that I kept during the debt-free journey (I secretly hate that phrase, can we please coin a new one).

In the time that I stayed at my part-time job after leaving the full-time job, I didn't keep the hours for the money. I kept the position because for the most part I genuinely liked it. It was a comfortable space.

But soon I wondered if I felt comfortable for the wrong reasons. I liked how it felt to do the work and be part of that company, but a part of me also felt I was holding myself back. Leaving that company was harder than my full-time job, but I don't regret it.

I think that means I'm still open to change, to growth, to leveling up in my life.

I'm also working on my next full-time source of income. It's daunting, but exciting. I've spent my whole adult life wishing I could find something I like to do that also pays money and I was fortunate to find it.

But fear of failing almost held me back. What if I made less money? What if I wasn't successful as quickly as I wanted to be? What if the other financial goals I set weren't achieved in the time I told myself they should be?

What if...

What if instead I stopped pressuring myself? What if I took a break and felt the positive effects of being debt-free? What if I spent more time enjoying life and less time setting money goals and comparing our Instagram updates to everyone else's?

Ah, but these weren't choices I had looked at before. They weren't even choices I knew I had.

Despite being debt-free, I had indoctrinated myself and spun a new narrative. I told myself a new story of what was expected of my life and what it had to be. We had to save "this much." We had to put "that much" into retirement. We had to take a certain vacation. I had to make "so much" money.

We couldn't slow down. *I* couldn't slow down.

But we had just given three years! Three years traded in order to be done! We did it then so we didn't have to do it later! What was I doing? Why was I convinced I always had to be chasing something?

There are ways to live abundantly and intentionally without being so obsessed with money and financial goals. It is possible to merge the two without going off the deep end.

That is my mission now.

Living life intentionally and successfully without either aspect being heavily dependent on or influenced by strict, extreme money goals.

It's hard. I'm not good at focusing on one small thing at a time. I like multitasking. I like going all out until it breaks me. There might be a time and place for it again, but it needs to happen for better reasons than being backed into a corner or because I told myself an inaccurate story.

If you are anything like me and you think this might be an issue (during any time of your life, regarding money or otherwise), I have discovered a few simple solutions that help me.

The first is to let go. Let go of the following heavy burdens:

Expectations: the ones you have for yourself and the ones you think other people have of you.

I knew that becoming debt-free was good for me and for our future. But there were times I felt I had to achieve it faster because I knew people were watching. They saw my updates, they talked to us about our schedules, and they knew what we were doing.

But not a single person ever said to me, "You should be done by December 2018." Or, "You should work more and be done by August 2018." I never heard an expectation voiced to me. I created them in my head. I imagined people were thinking these things (and if they were, who cares?) and I let it become a burden.

Pressures: the mental stress brought on by the situation and the tension that may truly be "all in your head."

I know I put extra unnecessary pressure on myself. Nobody said I had to work harder or sacrifice more. There was only one other person affected by my actions, and Jason always trusted me to decide what was right for me. Yes, he wanted the debt paid as badly and as fast as I did. But if we did all that we could, he was satisfied.

All the mental stress I felt was my own and only I could relieve it. I heard this once and it's stuck with me: "Everything you're carrying, you picked up."

Comparison. Social media is a heck of a thing. I can feel so connected to the world around me one second and completely alone and isolated the next. I feel motivated and inspired about life, but with one more thumb scroll I feel like I can't breathe because of the anxieties caused by insecurity and inadequacy.

"But it's all a highlight reel," we remind ourselves. Yes and no. It's becoming more common for people to post their lows as well. This isn't a bad thing, but it's still something we risk comparing ourselves to.

I loved posting our debt-free updates and goals. I liked interacting with other people through this tool and felt encouraged to keep going. But sometimes I followed other debt-free accounts and saw they paid more or they did it faster than we did, or I worked twelve hours and they worked fourteen.

Anything someone can do, someone else can do "better."

Don't follow the content that makes you feel small or inferior.

The second solution is to focus on today.

Somewhere along the way I stopped recognizing each day as its own piece of the present. I was all about the next paycheck and payment and was dreading all the future hours I needed to work, but I forgot that I wasn't living in those moments yet. I was living in one moment, for one day. What would come would come. I didn't need to squander what I was presently given.

I sabotaged my own mood when I wasn't paying attention. I dreaded the coming week, so I wasn't positive or fully present at a social gathering. I felt anxiety about waking up so early every morning and it kept me from falling asleep. I stressed about having to spend money and forgot I was living a life and that this life requires some guilt-free expenses.

I thought this problem would miraculously disappear when the debt was gone and I changed my work situation.

I'm sure you guessed it: it did not miraculously disappear.

As I'm typing this I'm going over the last few days and weeks, wondering how I've been doing in this area. (Some days, great; others, not so much.) I prepare for the week and I make plans for the month, but I need to focus on and recognize today. We should respect and be thankful for these twenty-four hours.

Recently the area I've needed to apply this focus is with our money and financial goals.

I get swept up in large, electrifying goals that are somewhat realistic but also based on hopes and assumptions about the future. I postulate we'll make a certain amount of money and spend a certain amount, and assume we should be able to save the rest.

But this turns into a goal I set in stone, accompanied by my frenemies: expectation, pressure, and comparison. If I find we can't meet the goal, I become disappointed, aimless, irrationally frustrated and irritated (with myself), and I wonder what I'm even doing with my life anyway.

Then I tried a new type of budgeting (or a new way to handle money, if you still aren't fond of the B word).

I mentioned before that I don't budget as intensely anymore. When we were at the height of our income while paying down debt, we knew we could budget loosely and remain accountable to our expenses and still succeed.

(Looking back, I wish I had handled this differently. I wish I had put even more effort into budgeting. Not because I think we could have become debt-free sooner, but because I want to know that I truly did all that I could during that time.)

But now that income we had has dropped. The situation has changed. When this happened I began to feel out of control, uncertain of what our money was doing when we weren't looking.

I also felt burned out on financial books and resources. *I know all this. I just did it. I'm still doing it. We have our stuff together now. There's nothing new to learn that applies to us.*

Remind me: How did I get caught up in our first notable money debacle? What caused that to happen the way it did? It was the evil debt! The lack of money!

"Not quite..." you're thinking.

It was me. It was my pride and my cocky attitude. It was thinking I knew everything and had it all figured out. History really does have the potential to repeat itself, doesn't it?

This new-to-me budgeting method isn't very different from the one I already followed, so I'm using it in addition to the zero-based budget. When I talked about the budgeting methods, I mentioned that no method is better than another if it accomplishes the goals you need it to. I don't believe this method is better than the one I used to do. I think the process I used served a purpose three years ago and that now I need a process that serves a different purpose.

Remember, that's the beauty and the power of personal finances: the personal part. I'm evaluating the parts of each method that meet my needs and connecting them in my process. I'm doing what works for *me*.

And even after I tell you about it it's important that you still only do what works for *you*.

I'm still doing a different budget each month and deciding where our money will go before it arrives. But instead of looking at it all together over the scope of a whole month, I'm breaking the process down by paycheck, which for us covers a two-week period.

Before the month starts I print out a calendar and write down each bill, expense, and budget category (this includes both the numbers I know for sure and the ones I'm estimating). I write down which Fridays have a paycheck and highlight each paycheck amount in a different color. Then I go down the calendar and mark each item, matching its color with the paycheck that will cover the amount.

When the paycheck hits our account, I write out what this paycheck is going to do. I write down only the expenses in that calendar time period and then write down what happens with the money that is leftover.

Sometimes the money goes directly into the twelve-month emergency fund we're building. Sometimes it goes into the sinking fund for our next car. Sometimes it stays in that account to be a buffer for unexpected expenses and spending.

Adding this system to a zero-based budget method has reduced my anxiety about our lower income. I can see on paper with real numbers that our bills will be covered. Our savings goals will be met. Our money will not go to waste.

But the most important part of this budget to me is that it's restoring my focus on the money we have in our account, not just the future money. It's reestablishing the importance of Today.

I'm focusing on today's money and what it needs to do for us. I'm appreciating the income we've earned and the life we're choosing and creating with it.

It's very simple. It's incredibly effective. The first time I did it, it felt pointless. I knew it all in my head. I knew when our bills were due. I knew we had enough to be able to put money into savings. I knew in my head that we were fine.

But after a few more times I saw the benefit to what I was doing: I felt I was in control. I knew it in my gut.

And then our money began to have meaning to me again.

It isn't just a number in the bank or a bill in my pocket. It's this week's gas, next week's electric bill, this year's Christmas, next year's vacation, and whatever else we tell it to be.

Giving so much extra money (and time) to the debt made me feel detached from our money. I had to handle it, but I couldn't grow fond of it. It wasn't ours to keep.

But now that has changed. We keep our money. We do what we want with it.

A day we work isn't just the number on the paycheck; it's our monthly subscriptions for TV and music or a birthday gift I'm buying for my best friend. It's the meal at our favorite restaurant and the extra tip for our waiter or waitress.

It's our guarantee for today and our hope for the future.

Connect with your money. Focus on its meaning and its place in your life.

Value the effort and time it took to earn it.

Forgive yourself when you part with more of it than was planned.

Change or create your money mindset.

Discover the power of personal finances.

Discover the power in *you. You can do this.* Success with money isn't just for the people who write the books about it. It's for everyone.

You can do something epic. You can fail and fall down a hundred times (maybe 105,000 times, like I feel I did) and still get back up.

Going into debt and facing a money mess can be awful, but it isn't the end of the world. There is always room to add more pages to your story.

P.S.

This whole book is about money and debt and the way we confronted and changed our personal finances.

But we both know it's about more than that: it's about how we changed our lives. How we changed our future and rewrote our story.

Writing this book was a metaphorical way to close out this chapter in my life. There are no more Instagram updates, no more loan payments, no more ninety-hour workweeks. People aren't messaging me about what we're doing, because as far as that story is concerned, we are done. We are debt-free.

At first, this was daunting. How could we top this? What could we do next that was just as exhilarating?

The reality is there may not be another financial task to complete that feels the way this process felt. Saving money is cool, traveling to a new country is fun, and retirement is worth looking forward to, but I have a feeling that for us there will be nothing else quite like the adrenaline rush of making a final loan payment or setting a crazy goal and beating it.

If that's the case, I think it's a good thing.

I think it's good that we have more to wake up for than a paycheck, or more to be thankful for than a Friday. I think it's healthy to have life goals without dollar signs and reasons to be proud of yourself that have nothing to do with your income.

Life is more than our greatest hits or our top financial achievements.

I'm really grateful about that, because, do you know what that means?

There is more to life than money.

I am learning ways
to count the reasons of my worth
with more than heavy coins that leave my skin colored with sadness
and old paper bills that crinkle and fall apart;
I used to bathe in them,
but now my skin is so dry, my meaning
<u>spent</u>

When we say count your blessings, we do not say – add them up
We do not say – the highest total wins
We say count them, name them, see them, admire them, learn from them,
give them away

And I am storing up reasons to keep breathing,
and you cannot buy that, you cannot sell it,
we cannot earn more breaths than the ones we already have,
I cannot pay for happiness,
I cannot take out a loan for grace.

I am more than my balance sheet,
I am more than the notes / the pounds / the signs / the currencies
we love to measure ourselves with...

...and, dear reader, so are you.

Resources

Books

The Total Money Makeover – Dave Ramsey

Be Obsessed or Be Average – Grant Cardone

You Need A Budget – Jesse Mecham

Money: Master the Game – Tony Robbins

Millionaire Teacher – Andrew Hallam

Your Money or Your Life (Revised for 2018) – Vicki Robin and Joe Dominguez

Programs / Websites

Financial Peace University

www.thebudgetmom.com

Apps

EveryDollar Easy Budgeting App

YNAB (You Need A Budget)

Fudget: Budget Planner Tracker

Tally – Pay Off Debt Faster

Twine: Easy Saving & Investing

Made in the
USA
Middletown, DE